3:16

THE CHURCH EXPERIENCE WORKBOOK

MAX LUCADO

With learning activities and leader guide by
JUDI HAYES, AMY MASON, STARLA SHATTLER,
JOE SNIDER, AMY SUMMERS, *and* MARK WHITLOCK

LifeWay Press®
Nashville, Tennessee

Published by LifeWay Press®
© 2007 Max Lucado

The primary text of this workbook was taken from *3:16 The Numbers of Hope*
by Max Lucado, © 2007 Max Lucado, published by Thomas Nelson, Inc.

ISBN 978-1-4158-6413-5
Item 005115511

This book is a resource in the subject area Church and Bible Studies
in the Christian Growth Study Plan.
Course CG-1321

Dewey Decimal Classification: 226.5
Subject Headings: BIBLE. N.T. JOHN 3:16—STUDY \ SALVATION

Unless otherwise noted, all Scripture quotations are taken from the New International Version ©
International Bible Publishers 1973, 1978, 1987. Used by permission. Scriptures identified NLT
are taken from the Holy Bible, New Living Translation, copyright © 1996. Used by permission of
Tyndale House Publishers, Inc., Wheaton, IL 60189 USA. All rights reserved. Scriptures identified
RSV are from the Revised Standard Version of the Bible, copyrighted 1946, 1952, © 1971, 1973.
Scriptures identified NKJV are from the New King James Version. Copyright © 1979, 1980, 1982,
Thomas Nelson, Inc., Publishers. Scriptures identified NCV are from the New Century Version®.
Copyright © 1987, 1988, 1991 by Thomas Nelson, Inc. Used by permission. All rights reserved.
Scriptures identified NASB are taken from the New American Standard Bible®, Copyright © 1960,
1962, 1963, 1968, 1971, 1972, 1973, 1975, 1977, 1995 by The Lockman Foundation. Used by
permission. *(www.lockman.org)* Scriptures identified MSG are from THE MESSAGE. Copyright
© by Eugene Peterson, 1993, 1994, 1995. Used by permission of NavPress Publishing Group.
Scriptures identified ESV are from the The Holy Bible, English Standard Version®, copyright ©
2001 by Crossway Bibles, a publishing ministry of Good News Publishers. Used by permission. All
rights reserved. Scriptures identified AMP are taken from The Amplified® Bible, copyright © 1954,
1958, 1962, 1964, 1965, 1987 by the Lockman Foundation. Used by permission. *(www.lockman.
org)* Scriptures identified NEB are from The New English Bible. Copyright © Oxford University
Press and Cambridge University Press, 1961, 1970. All rights reserved. Reprinted by permission.
Scriptures identified HCSB® are taken from the Holman Christian Standard Bible®,
copyright © 1999, 2000, 2002, 2003 by Holman Bible Publishers. Used by permission.

To order additional copies of this resource, write to LifeWay Church Resources Customer Service;
One LifeWay Plaza; Nashville, TN 37234-0113; fax order to (615) 251-5933; call toll free (800)
458-2772; order online at *www.lifeway.com;* e-mail *orderentry@lifeway.com;* or visit the LifeWay
Christian Store serving you.

Printed in the United States of America

Leadership and Adult Publishing
LifeWay Church Resources
One LifeWay Plaza
Nashville, TN 37234-0175

CONTENTS

Introducing Max Lucado. 4

Introducing 3:16 5

Week 1
A Parade of Hope 7

Week 2
God Loves 25

Week 3
God Gave. 49

Week 4
We Believe 69

Week 5
We Live 89

Week 6
God's Whoever Policy 115

The 3:16 Life. 133

3:16 Prayer List. 152

Leader Guide 154

Endnotes. 170

Christian Growth Study Plan 173

INTRODUCING MAX LUCADO

Since 1985 this Texas pastor has taken pen to paper, sharing his heart and his stories with readers around the globe. His books have been translated into more than 28 languages worldwide.

Max is one of the rare authors who can craft memorable books for readers of all ages, races, and creeds. He has written best-selling books for both children and adults, from illustrated storybooks to nonfiction and biblical commentary.

Yet all these books and products find their wellspring in a single source: the pulpit at Oak Hills Church in San Antonio, Texas. All of Max's books for adults have been birthed as sermons for the congregation at Oak Hills Church, where he has served for 20 years.

Max and Denalyn Lucado celebrated 26 years of marriage in August 2007. They served as missionaries in Brazil before coming to San Antonio, where they have lived since 1988. Their three almost-grown daughters (Jenna, Andrea, and Sara) recall no other home. Both the heart and the pen of this pastor/writer have found fertile ground under the Texas sun.

INTRODUCING 3:16

Welcome, friends.

We're beginning an exploration of one of the most important verses in the Bible. Before we dig into these words of hope, let's take a quick overview of this workbook. My friends at LifeWay have developed this curriculum for you to study with family, friends, and neighbors or with others at your church. Our goal: to understand the message and apply the truths of this verse to your life. Here's how the study works:

At the beginning of each week, you'll get together with a small group to view a video message on a portion of John 3:16. Following the message, your small group will be guided to respond to what you've heard. During the week, five daily devotionals will help you review that message, go deeper in your understanding, and apply it to your daily life. You will want to complete the devotional studies on your own before your next group meeting. Each day you will:

1 **Use the activities suggested. Their purpose is to help you learn and integrate the message into your life. Review the elements in this book listed in the margin on this page. Look at the sample on the pages indicated. When you've finished, place a check mark in this box:** ▦

Ponder your own life and how you relate to John 3:16. Those who will study this message fall into two categories. Some have

---

Examples of the Study Elements in 3:16 THE CHURCH EXPERIENCE

1. DVD listening guide (top of p. 9)
2. Small-Group Response, where you'll discuss what you heard (bottom of p. 9)
3. Preview of the week (both the focus in John 3:16 and highlights from the study, p. 10)
4. Daily devotionals (like day 1 on p. 11)
5. A prayer activity at the end of each day (bottom of p. 13)
6. 3:16 Prayer List (pp. 152–53)
7. Leader Guide with session plans for your group (pp. 154–69)
8. Review of the previous week's content (p. 26)

already believed in Jesus Christ and have accepted His free gift of eternal life. For others, learning about Jesus and His message of salvation is a new experience.

2 **Read the 3:16 promise in the margin. Which category would you use to describe your relationship to the John 3:16 promise? Check one.**
   a. I've already believed in Christ and deposited
       the 3:16 promise in my heart.
   b. I've not yet believed.

If you checked *a* above, the assignments in "The 3:16 Life" (pp. 133–51) will lead you to identify the ways Christ has made a difference in your life. The lessons will guide you to prepare and tell your 3:16 story. People you know and love need to know that John 3:16 is not just a two-thousand-year-old message for Nicodemus. It's alive in your life and can be in theirs. You'll be inspired by hearing others in your small group tell their 3:16 stories.

If you checked *b* above, studying John 3:16 will help you grasp the power of God's love and His purpose for your life. Choosing faith in Christ and following Him is the most important decision of your life. Our prayer is that God will reveal Himself to you in such a way that you will one day believe in Christ. Special activities in "The 3:16 Life" will help you think clearly and honestly about the significance of this verse.

Now let's begin our journey in New York City, where I'm introducing 3:16—the numbers of hope—to some great folks in The Bronx.

A PARADE OF HOPE

Week 1

INTRODUCING 3:16

Follow the session plans in the leader guide on page 158.

1. Introduce yourself to the group by sharing: (1) your name and brief information about your family; (2) where you spend most of your time during the week (home, school, business); and (3) why you chose to participate in this study.

2. We will study the parade of hope found in John 3:16, which stands in sharp contrast to times of fear, terror, loss, or despair. How did you feel when you received news of the terrorist attacks on September 11, 2001? Were you directly affected by the loss of a friend or a loved one and, if so, how?

3. Now briefly share memories of *one* of these other historic dark days:

- Attack of Pearl Harbor, *December 7, 1941*

- Assassination of John F. Kennedy, *November 22, 1963*

- Assassination of Martin Luther King, *April 4, 1968*

- Death of Elvis Presley, *August 16, 1977*

- Mount Saint Helens eruption, *May 18, 1980*

- Space Shuttle Challenger disaster, *January 28, 1986*

- San Francisco earthquake, *October 17, 1989*

- Oklahoma City bombing, *April 19, 1995*

- Death of Princess Diana, *August 31, 1997*

- Space Shuttle Columbia disaster, *February 1, 2003*

- Asian tsunami, *December 26, 2004*

- Hurricane Katrina, *August 23–31, 2005*

VIEW DVD MESSAGE: "A PARADE OF HOPE"

"For God so loved the world that he gave his one and only Son, that whoever believes in him shall not perish but have eternal life." John 3:16

1. 3:16 The Numbers of _____

2. The world is full of numbers of despair, numbers of confusion, numbers of fear.

3. Nine-one-one (9/11) … numbers of fear. God would like to replace them with 3:16—the numbers of hope.

4. A 26-word parade of hope: beginning with _____, ending with _____, and urging us to do the same.

5. He loves. He gave. We believe. We live.

6. _____ was John Newton's favorite word.

7. *Zoe*—the word that describes the _____ of God

8. Whoever stretches himself out on Him to _____ shall not perish but have everlasting life.

9. "My best prescription for head and heart is that *God so loved the world, that He gave His only begotten Son, that whosoever believeth in Him should not perish, but have everlasting life.*"—Martin Luther

Scripture referenced: John 3:16
Message-notes blanks: (1) Hope; (4) God, life; (6) Whoever; (7) life; (8) rest

GROUP RESPONSE

1. What are some of the reasons the world is so starved for hope? What are the things that most significantly rob the world of hope?

2. Which word snatched your attention during the slower reading of John 3:16 and why? *Loved, world, Son, whoever, life, believes,* or another?

3. "Life has letdowns." If you had to describe in one sentence the event or experience in life that most let you down, what would it be?

4. Optional: When and how did you deposit the 3:16 promise in your heart?

FOR GOD
SO LOVED
THE WORLD
THAT HE
GAVE HIS

ONE AND ONLY SON

THAT

WHOEVER
BELIEVES
IN HIM
SHALL NOT

PERISH

BUT HAVE
ETERNAL

LIFE.

JOHN 3:16

HIGHLIGHTS FOR WEEK 1

1. John 3:16 is—
   - a 26-word parade of hope: beginning with God, ending with life, and urging us to do the same;
   - the Continental Divide of Scripture, the international dateline of faith.
2. Jesus pounds Do Not Enter signs on every square inch of Satan's gate and tells those hell-bent on entering to do so over His dead body.

DON'T FORGET TO WORK ON YOUR 3:16 STORY IN DAY 5.

HOPE THAT DELIVERS

1 **If you have not already done so, read "Introducing 3:16" on pages 5–6 before starting today's devotional.**

One of the things you'll do in this study is share stories. Hopefully you're studying with a group of friends. Max will drop in by means of video. you'll remember the somewhat embarrassing episode of the $3.50 water bill refund. Max though he was about to receive a windfall and solve the world's problems.

Have you ever had a time when your expectations got away from you and you wound up disappointed? Some hopes fail to deliver. Some expectations sputter and flop like an untied balloon. Remember the shining-armor boyfriend who became the heartbreaking two-timer? The fast-track promotion that landed you in the forgotten basement cubicle? The cross-country move you made to "find yourself"? You found yourself, all right. You found yourself with higher rent and fewer friends.

SOME HOPES FAIL
TO DELIVER.

2 **Can you relate to this kind of disappointment? If so, describe your time of runaway expectations and disappointing results.**

_____

_____

_____

_____

3 **How has that disappointment affected your view of the world, your level of optimism and hope?**

_____

_____

_____

IF YOU KNOW
NOTHING OF THE
BIBLE, START HERE.

IF YOU KNOW
EVERYTHING IN THE
BIBLE, RETURN HERE.

Life has its letdowns, doesn't it? Hopes fail to deliver. But God has something we all desperately desire. In this journey together we're going to explore something we all need. It's a 26-word parade of hope: beginning with God, ending with life, and urging us to do the same. Brief enough to write on a napkin or memorize in a moment yet solid enough to weather two thousand years of storms and questions. If you know nothing of the Bible, start here. If you know everything in the Bible, return here. We all need the reminder. The heart of the human problem is the heart of the human. And God's treatment is prescribed in John 3:16:

God loves.   God gave.   We believe.   We live.

The verse is an alphabet of grace, a table of contents to Christian hope, each word a safe-deposit box of jewels: "For God so loved the world that he gave his one and only Son, that whoever believes in him shall not perish but have eternal life."

JOHN 3:16

"For God so loved the world that he gave his one and only Son, that whoever believes in him shall not perish but have eternal life."

4 **Do you need some hope right now? Hope for a job, a broken relationship, a wayward family member, financial provisions, a personal need or … ? What is one situation in which you could use some more hope?**

_____

_____

_____

_____

5 **Do you face any situation in which you are resisting hope because of fear?** ▪ Yes ▪ No If so, describe it here.

_____

_____

_____

YOUR CONVERSATION WITH GOD

As you've walked through this first day of the study, you've recalled times when your hopes were dashed, your future seemed bankrupt, and your expectations went unrealized. These moments are your personal ground-zero. Lay it out before God. Don't sweep it under the rug of the subconscious.

Amid the clamor of the day-to-day, we don't even acknowledge the deadness where hope used to live. The process stirs up emotions and memories just below the surface. Buried but still there. So what in your life smells of despair and hopelessness? Jesus said, "I am the resurrection and the life" (John 11:25). Ask Him to speak to the hopes you may have prematurely buried and to breathe life into them.

Lord Jesus, Son of God, You know the hopes that have grown cold in my life. I walk around them daily, secretly wishing to see them come to life again but fearing the disappointment I feel when my prayers aren't answered immediately or the way I want them answered. I confess my unbelief. Help me!

Right now I choose to hope in all things, even impossible things. I refuse to allow my fears and despair to rule over me. They are poor masters. Out of the ashes of my life, I believe You are the hope of my life. Deliver me, O God.

JOHN 3:1

"There was a man from the Pharisees named Nicodemus, a ruler of the Jews."

NICODEMUS

Pharisee, a Torah scholar, one of the 71 men on the Judean supreme court—the Sanhedrin

He's waiting for the shadows. Darkness will afford the cover he covets. So he waits for the safety of nightfall. He sits near the second-floor window of his house, sipping olive-leaf tea, watching the sunset, biding his time. Jerusalem enchants at this hour. The disappearing sunlight tints the stone streets, gilds the white houses, and highlights the blockish temple.

Nicodemus looks across the slate roofs at the massive square, gleaming and resplendent. He walked its courtyard this morning. He'll do so again tomorrow. He'll gather with religious leaders and do what religious leaders do: discuss God. Discuss reaching God, pleasing God, appeasing God.

Pharisees converse about God. And Nicodemus sits among them. Debating. Pondering. Solving puzzles. Resolving dilemmas. *Sandal tying on the Sabbath. Feeding people who won't work. Divorcing your wife. Dishonoring parents.*

1 **Why do you suppose we sometimes focus on religious trivia rather than on God?**

_____

_____

2 **Why do you think it's easier to follow a religious system than to follow Jesus? What's the difference?**

_____

_____

What does God say? Nicodemus needs to know. It's his job. He's a holy man and leads holy men. His name appears on the elite list of Torah scholars. He dedicated his life to the law and occupies one of the 71 seats on the Judean supreme court. He has credentials, clout, and questions.

More than anything, Nick has questions for this Galilean crowd-stopper. This backwater teacher who lacks diplomas yet attracts people. Who has ample time for the happy-hour crowd but little time for clergy and the holy upper crust. He banishes demons, some say; forgives sin, others claim.

3 Read the following Scripture. Underline the things Jesus did that disrupted the comfortable world of Nicodemus and the other religious leaders.

"Jesus went throughout Galilee, teaching in their synagogues, preaching the good news of the kingdom, and healing every disease and sickness among the people. News about him spread all over Syria, and people brought to him all who were ill with various diseases, those suffering severe pain, the demon-possessed, those having seizures, and the paralyzed, and he healed them. Large crowds from Galilee, the Decapolis, Jerusalem, Judea and the region across the Jordan followed him." Matthew 4:23-25

4 Read John 2:13-16 in the margin. How do you think the religious leaders would have felt toward Jesus for purging the temple? Check all that you think apply.

▪ a. Indignant. Challenged. "Who does He think He is?"

▪ b. Angry. Robbed. "He's cutting into our profits."

▪ c. Vengeful. "We've got to get rid of this renegade."

▪ d. Complacent. "Just a blip in the line of doing business."

JOHN 2:13-16

"When it was almost time for the Jewish Passover, Jesus went up to Jerusalem. In the temple courts he found men selling cattle, sheep and doves, and others sitting at tables exchanging money. So he made a whip out of cords, and drove all from the temple area, both sheep and cattle; he scattered the coins of the money changers and overturned their tables. To those who sold doves he said, 'Get these out of here! How dare you turn my Father's house into a market!'"

NICODEMUS
COMES AT NIGHT.
HIS COLLEAGUES
CAN'T KNOW OF
THE MEETING.
THEY WOULDN'T
UNDERSTAND.

So Nicodemus comes at night. His colleagues can't know of the meeting. They wouldn't understand. But Nicodemus can't wait until they do. As the shadows darken the city, he steps out, slips unseen through the cobbled, winding streets. He passes servants lighting lamps in the courtyards and takes a path that ends at the door of a simple house. Jesus and His followers are staying here, he's been told. Nicodemus knocks.

5 What internal struggles do you think drove Nicodemus to come to Jesus at night?
- a. He was seeking relief from hidden guilt.
- b. He didn't want to be seen.
- c. He thought others would misunderstand.
- d. He was just too busy during the day.
- e. Other: _____

6 Have you ever "come to Jesus at night"? If so, what drove you?

_____

_____

The room silences as Nicodemus enters. The wharf workers and tax collectors aren't used to the highbrow world of a scholar. Jesus motions for the guest to sit. Nicodemus does and initiates the most famous conversation in the Bible: "Rabbi, we know that You are a teacher come from God; for no one can do these signs that You do unless God is with him" (John 3:2, NKJV).

"RABBI, WE KNOW THAT YOU ARE A TEACHER COME FROM GOD."

7 "Rabbi" and "teacher come from God." Why do you think these titles are significant for Nicodemus?

_____

_____

Nicodemus begins with what he knows. *I've done my homework*, he implies. *Your work impresses me*. We listen for a kindred salutation from Jesus: "And I've heard of you, Nicodemus."

We expect some hospitable chitchat. None comes. Jesus makes no mention of Nicodemus's VIP status, good intentions, or academic credentials because, in Jesus' algorithm, they don't matter. He simply issues this proclamation: "Unless one is born again, he cannot see the kingdom of God" (v. 3, NKJV).

Behold the Continental Divide of Scripture, the international dateline of faith. Nicodemus stands on one side, Jesus on the other, and Christ pulls no punches about their differences.

The Continental
Divide of Scripture

Nicodemus inhabits a land of good efforts, sincere gestures, and hard work. Give God your best, his philosophy says, and God does the rest. Jesus responds: "Your best won't do. Your works don't work. Your finest efforts don't mean squat. Unless you are born again, you can't even see what God is up to."

YOUR CONVERSATION WITH GOD

To connect with Jesus, we must stop thinking of Him as an image on stained-glass windows. He was personal to Nicodemus and desires a personal relationship with you. Jesus is dying to—correction—*He died* to know you and for you to know Him.

Lord Jesus, I have often pursued You from a distance at night, but I realize I need and want You in the full light of day. I know that religion without relationship is tombstone dead. I confess my works aren't working and my effort to attain salvation is laughable. You ask me to surrender so that I can be born from You. And that's what I'm doing right now. So I'm coming to You, hands empty, in the light of day, heart wide open.

BORN AGAIN

Nicodemus hesitates on behalf of us all. Born again? "How can a man be born when he is old?" (John 3:4, NKJV). You must be kidding. Put life in reverse? Rewind the tape? Start all over? We can't be born again.

*"UNLESS ONE
IS BORN AGAIN ..."*

1 **What do you think of when you hear the words**
   born again?
   - A politician using God to improve his image
   - Someone caught in a crime escaping responsibility
   - An emotional experience
   - A mulligan, a do-over
   - Other: _____

Born again has become a buzzword in popular culture, embraced by some and ridiculed by others. Nicodemus had no hook on which to hang such thoughts. Let's try to clear away the debris of our day and examine Jesus' words as if for the first time. Consider that first word. *Born* ...

2 **Write in the margin your reactions to the following**
   statements about a birth.
   - A father saying to his infant, "Great work there, Little One."
   - A child clawing his or her way down the birth canal
   - A mother doing all the work of the delivery
   - A doctor telling the father to push

Born again. Birth, by definition, is a passive act. The enwombed child contributes nothing to the delivery. Postpartum celebrations applaud the work of the mother. No one lionizes the infant. Give the tyke a pacifier, not a medal. Mom deserves the gold. She exerts the effort. She pushes, agonizes, and delivers.

The mother pays the price of birth. She doesn't enlist the child's assistance or solicit his or her advice. Why would she? The baby can't even take a breath without umbilical help, much less navigate a path into new life. Nor, Jesus is saying, can we. Spiritual rebirthing requires a capable Parent, not an able infant.

3 **How do you react to the idea that you can no more work yourself to God than a baby can birth itself?**

_____

_____

Nicodemus marveled at this idea because he was steeped in teaching that we must work our way to God, but Jesus speaks a different language—not works born of men and women but a work done by God.

4 **Underline the phrases in Jeremiah 31:33-34 (margin) that point to God's accomplishing the work of new birth.**

Circle anything else you see in the prophecy of a new covenant that fits what Jesus told Nicodemus.

Bible students have long understood the new birth as a part of the new covenant of Jeremiah's prophecy. Look at some of the other references to the new covenant we see in Scripture.

- "I will give you a new heart and put a new spirit in you" (Ezek. 36:26).

JEREMIAH 31:33-34, HCSB

"'Instead, this is the covenant I will make with the house of Israel after those days'—the LORD's declaration. 'I will place My law within them and write it on their hearts. I will be their God, and they will be My people ... for they will all know Me, from the least to the greatest of them'—the LORD's declaration. 'For I will forgive their wrongdoing and never again remember their sin.'"

- "If anyone is in Christ, he is a new creation; the old has gone, the new has come!" (2 Cor. 5:17).
- "He [Jesus] said to them, 'This is My blood that establishes the covenant; it is shed for many'" (Mark 14:24, HCSB).
- "This will be My covenant with them, when I take away their sins" (Rom. 11:27, HCSB).

5 Birth costs a mother pain and labor. In the light of what you have read about the new covenant, what did the new birth cost Jesus?

_____

6 In the margin write what you would like to say if you simply talked to Jesus and told Him your feelings about what He has done to make the new birth possible.

Jesus told Nicodemus he must be *born*—that says God exerts the effort. Now let's consider the second part. What did He mean born *again*?

Because of the Greek word used in John 3:3, The Message translates the phrase *born again* as "born from above." The word Jesus chose clearly indicated that the source of being born again must be God.

We don't try again. We need not the muscle of self but a miracle of God. The thought coldcocks Nicodemus: "How can this be?" (John 3:9). Jesus answers by leading him to the Hope Diamond of the Bible:

The Hope Diamond
of the Bible

> For God so loved
> the world that he gave his one
> and only Son, that whoever believes
> in him shall not perish
> but have eternal
> life.

7 Read the rest of this famous conversation. Underline statements of particular interest to you.

"For God did not send his Son into the world to condemn the world, but to save the world through him. Whoever believes in him is not condemned, but whoever does not believe stands condemned already because he has not believed in the name of God's one and only Son. This is the verdict: Light has come into the world, but men loved darkness instead of light because their deeds were evil. Everyone who does evil hates the light, and will not come into the light for fear that his deeds will be exposed. But whoever lives by the truth comes into the light, so that it may be seen plainly that what he has done has been done through God." John 3:17-21

YOUR CONVERSATION WITH GOD

When we encounter Jesus, we realize there would never be enough do-overs to bring us up to His level. It's like jumping to the moon. But He came down to us. What an incredible truth! This reality of our desperation and His act of redemption drives us to worship Him with passion. Spend a few moments reflecting on the towering achievement of Jesus' life and incomprehensible death.

Lord Jesus, I am amazed by the gift of Your life for my freedom. Teach me to bask in Your unconditional love as I live life to the fullest. I am so thankful that You lived the life I could never live—perfect in all aspects. I'm amazed that You stretched out on a cross so that I could have life in all its unending beauty. Taking my place, taking my shame, all my imperfections, putting the world back together ... amazing!

THE 3:16 PROMISE

"GOD SO LOVED
THE WORLD …"

Let's take a big-picture look at this 3:16 promise. "God so loved the world …" We'd expect an anger-fueled God. One who punishes the world, recycles the world, forsakes the world … but loves the world?

The world? *This* world? Heartbreakers, hope-snatchers, and dream-dousers prowl this orb. Dictators rage. Abusers inflict. Reverends think they deserve the title.

1 **What do you think is the most unlovable thing about this world?**

_____

2 **Now let me ask a much harder question: what do you think is the most unlovable thing about yourself?**

_____

GOD GAVE HIS SON
… HIS ONLY SON.

But God still loves. He loves the world so much that He gave His: Declarations? Rules? Dicta? Edicts? No. The heart-stilling, mind-bending, deal-making-or-breaking claim of John 3:16 is this: *God gave His Son … His only Son.*

Go back to the questions for a moment. He gave His only Son for the worst of the world and the worst of you and me. No abstract ideas but a flesh-wrapped divinity. Scripture equates Jesus with God. God, then, gave Himself. Why? So that "whoever believes in him shall not perish."

3 **For the world at large, what do you think is the most common perception about God? Check one and explain your answer in the margin.**
- a. Harsh, angry with sinners, condemning, judgmental
- b. Gentle, loving, forgiving, caring, self-sacrificing

4 **John Newton was a wicked sailor and slave trader before he came to trust Christ. Read the first verse of "Amazing Grace" in the margin. Why do you think John 3:16 inspired Newton to describe God's grace as amazing?**

_____

_____

AMAZING GRACE
Amazing grace! how sweet
　the sound,
That saved a wretch like me!
I once was lost, but now
　am found,
Was blind, but now I see.
—*John Newton*

Whoever …

When you know all you deserve is to perish because of your wicked life, and God says, "whoever believes … has eternal life"—that's *amazing* grace! *Whoever* … a universal word. And *perish* … a sobering word. We'd like to dilute, if not delete, the term. Not Jesus. He pounds Do Not Enter signs on every square inch of Satan's gate and tells those hell-bent on entering to do so over His dead body. Even so, some souls insist.

In the end some perish and some live. And what determines the difference? Not works or talents, pedigrees or possessions. Nicodemus had these in hoards. The difference is determined by our belief. "Whoever believes in him shall not perish but have eternal life."

5 **Would you say that your internal life is more characterized by rest or by work? Explain in the margin.**

You'll remember the story about the Bible translator who finally translated *believe* as *stretch himself out on Christ*. Jesus also said, "Are you tired? Worn out? Burned out on religion? Come to me. Get away with me and you'll recover your life. I'll show you how to take a real rest" (Matt. 11:28, MSG).

6 How would you explain to a friend what it means to stretch out on Christ and rest?

_____

_____

STRETCH OUT ON
CHRIST AND REST.

Stretch out on Christ and rest. As things turned out, Nicodemus did. When Jesus was crucified, the theologian showed up with Joseph of Arimathea. They offered their respects and oversaw Jesus' burial. When word hit the streets that Jesus was out of the tomb and back on His feet, don't you know Nicodemus smiled and thought of his late-night chat?

7 Who do you know who needs this 3:16 promise? Turn to the 3:16 Prayer List on page 152 and begin making a list of people who need to be born again.

Your Conversation with God

Reflect on the world God loved. Allow Him to reveal the enormity of the world's problems. In the midst of our mess, Jesus meets us where we are. The world is in a continual state of brokenness and messiness. And Jesus died for this? Yes, He did. For "whoever"!

Lord Jesus, Son of God, even the word whoever *brings me to worship. The very fact that You see everything ... and love me still. The fact that You love me despite all the crooked paths and false perceptions I carry around with me is almost too much to comprehend. Such knowledge is too great! Thank You for loving the ragamuffins, the outcasts, the slave traders, and yes, even me.*

FOR DAY 5 *turn to "The 3:16 Life" on page 134 and follow the instructions for week 1.*

GOD LOVES

Week 2

GROUP REVIEW OF WEEK 1

Follow the session plans in the leader guide on page 160.

1. Briefly describe a time you got lost at night. What were the circumstances, and how did you feel?

2. What's the difference between following a religious system and following Jesus? Share some of your thoughts from day 2, activity 2 (p. 14).

3. Nicodemus faced risks and struggles in coming to Jesus, just as many people do today. In your opinion, what drove Nicodemus to come to Jesus by night? Similarly, what might drive you and others to "come to Jesus at night" (day 2, activities 5 and 6, p. 16)?

4. What would you say if you had the opportunity to tell Jesus how much His work of the new birth means to you? Start with the ideas you jotted down in the margin for activity 6 on day 3 (p. 20).

5. On day 4 we recalled John Newton's dramatic life transformation. Why do you think John 3:16 inspired Newton to describe God's grace as "amazing" (activity 4, p. 23)? As you feel free to do so, share a time when God absolutely amazed you with His grace.

VIEW DVD MESSAGE: "GOD LOVES"

1. "Plutoed"—demoted or demeaned like the former planet Pluto. One day you're in, and the next day you're out.

2. God's love: you cannot _____ it.

3. *Hashaq* (huh-SHOCK)—to be tethered to, _____ to.

> O love that wilt not let me go,
>
> I rest my weary soul in Thee;
>
> I give Thee back the life I owe,
>
> That in Thine ocean depths its flow
>
> May richer, fuller be.—George Matheson

4. We do step out of God's plan, but we never step out of God's love.

5. God's love: you cannot _____ it.

6. *Agape* (ah-GAH-pay)—is less affection and more a _____,
   less a feeling and more an action.

7. God's love: you can _____ it.

8. One word of love from God offsets all the words of hurt and hate from others.

Scriptures referenced: John 3:16; Deuteronomy 10:15; Deuteronomy 7:7-8; Hosea 3:1; Ephesians 5:2
Message-notes blanks: (2) win; (3) attached; (5) lose; (6) decision; (7) refuse

GROUP RESPONSE

1. What are some ways we try to win or earn God's love?

2. What might we do to cause us to think that we have lost God's love?

3. What are the implications of being "tethered" to God by His love? Explain.

4. I shared several examples of *agape* love: a husband's love for an invalid wife;
   a father's love for his invalid son; Pop's blessing for his granddaughter; my
   relationship with my dog, Salty. Which one touched you most and why?

5. Optional sharing: Describe a time in your life when you experienced God's
   hashaq or *agape* love.

FOR GOD
SO LOVED
THE WORLD
THAT HE
GAVE HIS
ONE AND ONLY SON
THAT
WHOEVER
BELIEVES
IN HIM
SHALL NOT
PERISH
BUT HAVE
ETERNAL
LIFE.
JOHN 3:16

HIGHLIGHTS FOR WEEK 2

1. Our universe is God's preeminent missionary: "The heavens declare the glory of God" (Ps. 19:1).
2. The One who formed you pulls for you.
3. God loves Israel and the rest of us Plutos because He chooses to.
4. You live in a hard world, but you don't have to live with a hard heart.

DON'T FORGET TO WORK ON YOUR 3:16 STORY IN DAY 5.

PART TWO

"FOR GOD ..."

If only I could talk to the pilot. Thirty seconds would do. Face-to-face. Just an explanation. He was, after all, the one bumping my wife and me from his plane.

Not that I could blame him. Denalyn had picked up more than souvenirs in Hong Kong. She was so nauseous I had to push her through the airport in a wheelchair. She flopped onto her seat and pillowed her head against the window, and I promised to leave her alone for the 14-hour flight.

I had a simple goal: get Denalyn on the plane.

The airline staff had an opposite one: get Denalyn off.

Fault me for their fear. When a concerned flight attendant inquired about my wife's condition, I sent shock waves through the fuselage with my answer: "Virus." Attendants converged on our seats like police at a crime scene. Presidential news conferences have stirred fewer questions.

"How long has she been sick? Did you see a doctor?"

"Have you considered swimming home?"

I downplayed Denalyn's condition. "Give us one barf bag, and we're happy travelers." No one laughed. Apparently, bug-bearing patrons compete with terrorists for the title "Most Unwanted Passenger." The *virus* word reached the pilot, and the pilot rendered his verdict: "Not on my plane."

"You must leave," his bouncer informed matter-of-factly.

"Says who?"

"The pilot."

Bumped by the Pilot

I leaned sideways and looked down the aisle for the man in charge, but the cockpit door was closed. Coward. If only I could talk to him, present my side. We didn't deserve banishment. We pay our taxes, vote in primaries, tip waiters. I wanted to plead my case, but the man in charge was unavailable for comment. He had a 747 to fly, seven thousand miles to navigate … and no time for us.

A few disheartening minutes later Denalyn and I found ourselves back at the gate, making plans to spend an extra night in China. As an airline representative made a list of hotel phone numbers, I noticed the plane pulling away. Hurrying over to the airport window, I stared into the cockpit, hoping for a glimpse of the mystery aviator. I waved both arms and mouthed my request: "Can we talk?" He didn't stop. I never saw his face. (But if you're reading this page, sir or ma'am, perhaps we could chat?)

1 **Can you relate? Would you describe a time when you felt barred, discarded, rejected, or overlooked?**

_____

2 **Have you ever felt like you'd fallen off God's radar screen? If so, what is your typical internal dialogue?**

- a. God is too busy for me.
- b. I must have done something wrong for Him not to respond.
- c. His decisions scare me.
- d. My calls go unheard.
- e. I don't really matter.
- f. God has vacated the pilot's seat.

3:16 …
NO BIBLE VERSE BETTER EXPRESSES HIS NATURE.

Christ weighs in decidedly on this discussion. He escorts passengers to the cockpit, enters 3:16 in the keypad, and unlocks the door to God. No Bible verse better expresses His nature. (We ought to submit it to Webster's.) Every word in the passage explains the second one. "For _God_ so loved the world …" (emphasis added).

3 **Have you asked God tough questions? Check the questions you have asked one time or another.**

- ▪ a. God, are You really engaged?
- ▪ b. Do You really notice or care about me?
- ▪ c. Are You harsh and judgmental or loving and merciful?
- ▪ d. How can You care about this messed-up world?

Other: _____

In John 3:16 Jesus assumes what Scripture declares: God is. Our universe is God's preeminent missionary: "The heavens declare the glory of God" (Ps. 19:1). A house implies a builder; a painting suggests a painter. Don't stars suggest a Star Maker? Doesn't creation imply a Creator? Look above you.

JESUS ASSUMES WHAT SCRIPTURE DECLARES: GOD IS.

4 **Did you know the Bible mentions many parts of outer space? Mark these statements *T* (true) or *F* (false).**

- ___ 1. The planet Venus is mentioned in the Bible.
- ___ 2. The planet Saturn is mentioned in the Bible.
- ___ 3. The Bible talks about the constellation Orion and a cluster of stars, Pleiades, twice.

Lee Strobel, an award-winning former legal editor for the *Chicago Tribune,* was an avowed atheist until he began to examine the evidence for God. His book *The Case for the Creator* demonstrates that whether you look through a telescope or a microscope, the scientific evidence for God is overwhelming.[1]

5 **What do you think the order and precision of nature reveals about God and His character?**

_____

_____

_____

_____

#4 answers: all true.
1. Isaiah 14:12;
2. Amos 5:26;
3. Job 38:31; Amos 5:8

6 Take your Bible discovery outside tonight. Using a star map (if you have one), look at the sky God paints for you tonight. While you marvel at the sky, meditate on Psalm 19. Jot notes about your experience in the margin. Here are a few of the verses from Psalm 19:

The heavens declare the glory of God;
the skies proclaim the work of his hands.
In the heavens he has pitched a tent for the sun,
which is like a bridegroom coming forth from his pavilion,
like a champion rejoicing to run his course.
It rises at one end of the heavens
and makes its circuit to the other;
nothing is hidden from its heat. Psalm 19:1,4-6

YOUR CONVERSATION WITH GOD

How do you speak to a God who created the Grand Canyon and the flea? Where does such a conversation start? Perhaps with the knowledge that the endlessly powerful, creative force has a name. He knows everything about you and still loves you. Meditate on the nature of Creator God.

Lord Jesus, God's only Son, I cease my self-congratulatory posture when I stop and think of all You are and evermore will be. I am amazed by Your power. I'm overwhelmed that I'm a part of this rich panorama of life. My soul craves to know how I fit into Your story. I shudder to think of the times I denied Your presence through self-preoccupation.

I have often shuffled sideways to avoid You without realizing the absurdity of my actions. Hold me in Your hands because it's true. I am weak, but You are strong.

No One like Him

We've looked to the heavens to see our Creator's fingerprints. Now look within you at your sense of right and wrong, your code of ethics. Somehow even as a child you knew it was wrong to hurt people and right to help them. What is this magnetic pole that pulls the needles on the compass of your conscience if not God?

We may violate or ignore the conscience, but we can't deny it. Even people who have never heard God's name sense His law within them: "There is something deep within [humanity] that echoes God's yes and no, right and wrong" (Rom. 2:15, MSG).

WHAT IS THIS MAGNETIC POLE THAT PULLS THE NEEDLES ON THE COMPASS OF YOUR CONSCIENCE IF NOT GOD?

1 **Identify the items below as virtues or evils. Write a *V* beside virtues and an *E* beside evils.**

___ Courage	___ Dishonesty	___ Compassion
___ Justice	___ Murder	___ Incest
___ Selfishness	___ Theft	___ Self-sacrifice
___ Heroism	___ Bribery	___ Humility

2 **You are seeking to convince a friend that God exists and cares for him. How would you explain that our sense of right and wrong argues for the existence of God.**

_____

_____

_____

1. Job 36:26—*"The number of His years is unsearchable"* (NASB).

2. Psalm 74:16—*"The day is yours, and yours also the night."*

3. Psalm 9:2—*"Before the mountains were brought forth, / Or ever You had formed the earth and the world, / Even from everlasting to everlasting, / You are God"* (NKJV).

4. Isaiah 6:3—*"Holy, holy, holy is the LORD of hosts"* (NKJV).

5. Isaiah 40:18—*"To whom, then, will you compare God?"*

6. Isaiah 46:9—*"I am God, and there is none like me."*

7. John 5:26—*"The Father has life in himself."*

8. Acts 17:25—*"Human hands can't serve his needs—for he has no needs"* (NLT).

9. Romans 16:26—He is *"the eternal God."*

10. James 1:13—*"God is impervious to evil"* (MSG).

3 **Have you ever tried to explain away or deny your conscience? How does our society justify doing so?**

_____

_____

When atheists decry injustice, they can thank God for the ability to discern it. The conscience is God's fingerprint, proof of His existence. It points us to the holiness of God. From all eternity He has never messed up. Every decision, exact. Each word, appropriate. Never out-of-bounds or out of place. Not even tempted to make a mistake: "God is impervious to evil" (Jas. 1:13, MSG).

4 **Match the Scriptures in the margin with the attributes of God below. Write a letter beside each number.**

a. Incomparable   ____ 1. Job 36:26

b. Self-sufficient   ____ 2. Psalm 74:16

c. Eternal   ____ 3. Psalm 90:2

d. Holy   ____ 4. Isaiah 6:3

____ 5. Isaiah 40:18

____ 6. Isaiah 46:9

____ 7. John 5:26

____ 8. Acts 17:27

____ 9. Romans 16:26

____ 10. James 1:13

But is God's grandness good news? When Isaiah saw it, he came unraveled: "Woe is me, for I am undone!" (Isa. 6:5, NKJV). Competent pilots boot sick people off the plane. An all-powerful God might do the same. Shouldn't the immensity of God intimidate us? Shouldn't we be overcome with pessimism?

In the cockpit: God, who has no needs, age, or sin. Bouncing around in the back of the plane: Max. Burger dependent. Half asleep. Compared to God, I have the life span of a fruit fly. And

(#4 answers: 1-c; 2-c; 3-c; 4-d; 5-a;
6-a; 7-b; 8-b; 9-c; 10-d)

sinless? I can't maintain a holy thought for my two-minute morning commute.

Is God's greatness good news? Not without the next four words of John 3:16: "For God *so loved the world*" (emphasis added).

Try that mantra on for size. The One who holds the aces holds your heart. The One who formed you pulls for you. Untrumpable power stoked by unstoppable love. "If God is for us, who can be against us?" (Rom. 8:31).

5 **Say the following phrases out loud:** *The One who holds the aces holds my heart. The One who formed me pulls for me.*

6 **What is the difference between believing God is *with* you and believing God is *for* you?**

_____
_____
_____

How would the two different beliefs play out in a person's emotions and actions?

_____
_____
_____

7 **I've listed in the margin some of the attributes of God— words describing His nature and character. Slowly read through that list and circle the ones that best state for you just how great and wonderful He is.**

GOD'S ATTRIBUTES

self-existent, unchangeable, mighty, powerful, providing, healing, dependable, sanctifying, peaceful, righteous, shepherding, present, all-sufficient, sovereign, all-seeing, everlasting, strong, all-knowing, all-powerful, changeless, eternal, faithful, glorious, good, holy, just, loving, majestic, merciful, omnipresent, righteous, perfect, infinite, gracious, patient, creative

Bill Tucker was 16 years old when his dad suffered a health crisis and had to leave his business. Even after Mr. Tucker regained his health, the Tucker family struggled financially, barely getting by.

Mr. Tucker, an entrepreneurial sort, came up with an idea. He won the bid to reupholster the chairs at the local movie theater. This stunned his family. He'd never stitched a seat. He didn't even own a sewing apparatus. Still, he found someone to teach him the skill and located an industrial-strength machine. The family scraped together every cent they had to buy it. They drained savings accounts and dug coins out of the sofa. Finally, they had enough.

It was a fine day when Bill rode with his dad to pick up the equipment. Bill remembers a jovial, hour-long trip discussing the bright horizons this new opportunity afforded them. They loaded the machine in the back of their truck. Mr. Tucker then invited his son to drive home. I'll let Bill tell you what happened:

"As we were driving along, we were excited, and I, like any sixteen-year-old driver, was probably not paying enough attention to my speed. As we were turning on the cloverleaf to get on the expressway, I will never forget watching that sewing machine begin to tip. I slammed on the brakes, but it was too late. I saw it go over the side. I jumped out and ran around the back of the truck. As I rounded the corner, I saw our hope and our dream lying on its side in pieces. Then I saw my dad just looking. All of his risk and all of his struggling and all of his dream, all of his hope to take care of his family was lying there, shattered.

"You know what comes next, don't you? 'Stupid, punk kid driving too fast, not paying attention, ruined the family by taking away our livelihood.' But that's not what he said. He looked right at me. 'Oh, Bill, I am so sorry.' And he walked over, put his arms around me, and said, 'Son, this is going to be okay.' " [2]

8 Have you ever done something stupid (intentionally or accidently) that caused you to feel guilt, shame, or regret? Something that caused a hopeless feeling inside of *This can't be fixed?* If so, in the margin write a word, initials, or a phrase that will remind you of that time.

"HE WALKED OVER, PUT HIS ARMS AROUND ME, AND SAID, 'SON, THIS IS GOING TO BE OKAY.'"

God is whispering to you what Bill Tucker's dad said to him. Those are God's arms you feel. Trust Him. That is His voice you hear. Believe Him. Allow the only decision maker in the universe to comfort you. Life at times appears to fall to pieces and seems irreparable. But it's going to be OK. How can you know? Because God so loved the world. And since He has no needs, you cannot tire Him. Since He is without age, you cannot lose Him. Since He has no sin, you cannot corrupt Him.

If God can make a billion galaxies, can't He make good from our bad and sense from our faltering lives? Of course He can! He is God. He not only flies the plane but also knows the passengers and has a special place for those who are sick and ready to get home.

YOUR CONVERSATION WITH GOD

Meditate on the reality that every person has faults, moral lapses, and slip-ups. Everyone with one exception: Jesus Christ. The One who was and is worthy. The Only Son of God. Do you have regrets about your thoughts, attitudes, and actions? Confess these to God. Confess that you are desperately in need of grace.

SINCE HE HAS NO NEEDS, YOU CANNOT TIRE HIM.

SINCE HE IS WITHOUT AGE, YOU CANNOT LOSE HIM.

SINCE HE HAS NO SIN, YOU CANNOT CORRUPT HIM.

Lord Jesus, Righteous One, I am so far from the standard. I confess that I need a covering. I'm not self-sufficient. I'm not clean. I am completely and utterly dependent on Your holiness, Your sufficiency, Your glory. So today I run to You because You are all I'm not and You've invited me to come and lay every silly, dysfunctional, self-sustaining idea I've ever invented at Your feet.

"SO LOVED"

HASHAQ

Hebrew word meaning "to be tethered to, attached to"

"For God so *loved* the world ..." (emphasis added). The fourth word in our parade of hope is *loved*. In our video time together we discussed two of the terms God employed to describe His love.

God loves us with a love that means He binds, or tethers, Himself to us. When the Hebrews heard Deuteronomy 10:15, they heard God say "The Lord binds *[hashaq]* Himself to His people." I told about a mom connected by a child harness to her rambunctious five-year-old.

1 **When you think of being tethered or bound to God, what ideas come to mind? Check all that apply or write your own.**

- Big Brother
- Intimacy
- Can't wander off
- Security
- Close
- Restriction
- Connected
- Micromanagement
- Control freak
- Loved
- Dictator
- Linked together
- Other: _____

2 **What part of being tethered to God gives you comfort and what part of the idea troubles you?**

Comforts me: _____

_____

Troubles me: _____

_____

3 Do you remember a time when the tether of God's love pulled you out of harm's way? If so, record it below.

_____

_____

4 Do you recall a time when God allowed you so much rope on your tether that you suffered negative results? If so, how does that affect your feelings about God's love?

_____

_____

GOD CHOOSES TO LOVE YOU

In the New Testament *hashaq* is replaced with the Greek *agape*, but the meaning is equally powerful. "God so *[agapao]* the world." *Agape* love is less an affection, more a decision; less a feeling, more an action. One linguist describes *agape* love as "an exercise of the Divine will in deliberate choice, made without assignable cause save that which lies in the nature of God Himself."[3] God's *agape* love does not mean an absence of intense feelings. It means God does more than simply feel warm emotions for us.

AGAPE

Greek word for love that is less affection and more a decision, less a feeling and more an action

5 Mark the following true or false based on God's *agape*.
___ 1. God loves me because I've impressed Him.
___ 2. God has chosen to love me in spite of my past because His nature is love.
___ 3. *Agape* means God doesn't feel strong emotion for me.
___ 4. *Agape* means God feels a full range of emotions but acts in a loving way toward me.

(#5 answers: 1. false; God's love is unconditional; 2. true; 3. false; God feels but does not allow His behavior to us to be governed by His feelings; 4. true)

6 How do you react to the idea that God loves you just as much, no matter what you do?

_____

_____

7 Love is active and at work. As you read the following verses, underline what love does or how God uses love in our lives. I've underlined the first one for you.

1. *"My command is this: Love each other as I have loved you. Greater love has no one than this, that he <u>lay down his life</u> for his friends."* John 15:12-13

2. *"God has poured out his love into our hearts by the Holy Spirit, whom he has given us… God demonstrates his own love for us in this: While we were still sinners, Christ died for us."* Romans 5:5-8

3. *"I am convinced that neither death nor life, neither angels nor demons, neither the present nor the future, nor any powers, neither height nor depth, nor anything else in all creation, will be able to separate us from the love of God that is in Christ Jesus our Lord."* Romans 8:38-39

4. *"I pray that you, being rooted and established in love, may have power, together with all the saints, to grasp how wide and long and high and deep is the love of Christ, and to know this love that surpasses knowledge—that you may be filled to the measure of all the fullness of God."* Ephesians 3:17-19

5. *"We know and rely on the love God has for us. God is love. Whoever lives in love lives in God, and God in him. In this way, love is made complete among us so that we will have confidence on the day of judgment, because in this world we are like him. There is no fear in love. But perfect love drives out fear, because fear has to do with punishment. The one who fears is not made perfect in love."* 1 John 4:16-18

(Phrases you might have underlined in question 7: lay down his life, poured out his love, demonstrates, separate us from, rooted and established in, surpasses knowledge, rely on, made complete, is no fear, drives out fear)

8 Draw a star beside the Scripture on the previous page that for you is the most meaningful description of God's love. Draw a circle beside the one most difficult for you to believe. Briefly explain why in the margin beside each.

9 Read aloud the following quotation by C. S. Lewis. He was commenting on 1 John 4:16-18 (p. 40).

"Perfect love, we know, casteth out fear. But so do several other things—ignorance, alcohol, passion, presumption, and stupidity. It is very desirable that we should all advance to that perfection of love in which we shall fear no longer; but it is very undesirable, until we have reached that stage, that we should allow any inferior agent to cast out our fear." [4]

10 What substitutes for love (if any) have you used to cast out fear in your life (for example, ignorance, alcohol, passion, presumption, stupidity)?

_____
_____
_____
_____
_____
_____

GOD'S LOVE ...

1. You cannot win it.

2. You cannot lose it.

3. You can refuse it.

Your goodness can't win God's love. Nor can your badness lose it. But you can refuse it. You can resist it. We tend to do so honestly. Having been Plutoed so often, we fear God may Pluto us as well. Rejections have left us skittish and jumpy.

Here's where I appeal to you. Don't settle for substitutes. Nothing can do for you what God's love was intended to do. Mark it down: God loves you with an unearthly love. You can't win it by being winsome. You can't lose it by being a loser. But you can be blind enough to resist it.

Don't. For heaven's sake, don't. For your sake, don't.

"Take in with all followers of Jesus the extravagant dimensions of Christ's love. Reach out and experience the breadth! Test its length! Plumb the depths! Rise to the heights! Live full lives, full in the fullness of God" (Eph. 3:18-19, MSG). Others demote you. God claims you. Let the definitive voice of the universe say, "You're still a part of My plan."

YOUR CONVERSATION WITH GOD

As you consider the depth of God's love, recall the times when you sensed God expressing His love toward you. You may not have even known it at the time. A sunset, a sudden brief encounter of grace, the smile of your firstborn child … celebrate those small epiphanies of divine love. Worship the Author of great love.

Lord Jesus, Lover of my soul, I tend to compare Your love to the love of people, and I forget that Your love is broader, deeper, stronger, and greater than anything I will ever experience. Indeed I have been loved—but not like this. I want to learn how to love people the way You so love me. Let this resounding love shake the foundation of my world. May Your love devastate the walls I've built to keep me safe. I surrender to love. Thank You, Jesus!

"THE WORLD"

"I saw a woman today who finally became hard as wood all over." French physician Guy Patin wrote these words in 1692, the first clinical description of fibrodysplasia ossificans progressiva, or FOP. He unknowingly introduced the world to a cryptic disease that slowly, irreversibly turns its victims into a mass of solid bone.

Healthy skeletal systems are hinged together with ligaments and tendons. FOP, however, hardens the soft tissues rendering the body an ossified suit of armor. Injuries often trigger the FOP sprawl. The body reacts in a predictable and devastating pattern: neck and spine solidify first, then shoulders, hips, and elbows. Over years the disease can imprison the entire body: back to front, head to toe, proximal to distal. The rogue gene of FOP has one aim: harden the body a little more every day.[5]

As tragic as this disease is, Scripture describes one even worse. The calcification not of the bones but of the will.

God spoke the following words to Moses on Mount Sinai. "I look at this people—oh! what a stubborn, hard-headed people!" (Ex. 32:9, MSG).

The disloyalty of the calf-worshiping Hebrews stunned God. He had given them a mayor's-seat perch at His exodus extravaganza. They saw water transform into blood, high noon change to a midnight sky, the Red Sea turn into a red carpet, and the Egyptian army become fish bait. God gave manna with the morning dew, quail with the evening sun. He earned their trust. The former slaves had witnessed a millennium of miracles in a matter of days.

FOP

Fibrodysplasia ossificans progressiva

THE FORMER SLAVES
HAD WITNESSED
A MILLENNIUM
OF MIRACLES IN
A MATTER OF DAYS.

43

1 Can you match the need of the Israelites on the left with the correct miracle of God on the right? Give it a try. Write a letter beside the number.

___ 1. Slavery	a. The waters return.
___ 2. Pharaoh's resistance	b. The promised land
___ 3. Homeless	c. Pillar of fire and a cloud
___ 4. Trapped at Red Sea	d. Moses to lead them out
___ 5. A pursuing army	e. Manna/quail
___ 6. Direction	f. 10 plagues
___ 7. Hunger	g. Water from a rock
___ 8. Thirst	h. Wind to part the waters

(#1 answers: 1-d; 2-f; 3-b; 4-h; 5-a; 6-c; 7-e; 8-g)

Mighty miracles ... and yet, when God called Moses to a summit meeting, the people panicked like henless chicks: "They rallied around Aaron and said, 'Do something. Make gods for us who will lead us. That Moses, the man who got us out of Egypt—who knows what's happened to him?'" (Ex. 32:1, MSG).

The scurvy of fear infected everyone in the camp. They crafted a metal cow and talked to it. God, shocked at the calf-praising service, commanded Moses, "Go! Get down there! ... They've turned away from the way I commanded them ... Oh! what a stubborn, hard-headed people!" (vv. 7-9, MSG).

2 Can you think of times when any of the following attitudes would have described you? Check all that apply.

- Hard-hearted
- Hardheaded
- Hard-nosed
- Hard to get along with
- Hard to get to know
- Hard of hearing
- Hard-boiled
- Hard to find

FOP spreads in an unhealthy response to injury. Our hearts harden in an unhealthy reaction to fear. Note: the presence of fear in the Hebrews didn't bother God; their response to it did. Nothing persuaded the people to trust Him. Plagues didn't. Liberation from slavery didn't. God shed light on their path and dropped food in their laps, and still nothing penetrated their hearts.

More than three thousand years removed, we understand God's frustration. We opt for more sophisticated therapies: belly-stretching food binges or budget-busting shopping sprees. We bow before a whiskey bottle or lose ourselves in an 80-hour work week. We still face fears without facing God.

3 **Most of us have our golden calves—a preferred drug of choice, so to speak. How do you tend to respond to stress, fear, loneliness, or pain? Check all that apply.**

- Ice cream
- Sexual immorality
- Overwork
- Illicit drugs
- Alcohol
- Pornography
- Partying, clubbing

- Nonstop television
- Churchaholism
- Prescription medications
- Shopping
- Sleep
- Internet surfing
- Exercise or sports

Others: _____

_____

_____

4 **What evidences of God's care and involvement do you need to recall in the times when God seems distant as He did to Israel?**

_____

_____

_____

_____

_____

_____

_____

According to heaven's medical diagnosis, hard-hearted people "are hopelessly confused. Their minds are full of darkness; they wander far from the life God gives because they have closed their minds and hardened their hearts against him. They have no sense of shame. They live for lustful pleasure and eagerly practice every kind of impurity (Eph. 4:17-19, NLT).

Measure the irregular pulse of the hard heart:

- "Hopelessly confused"
- "Minds ... of darkness"
- "Have no sense of shame"
- "Live for lustful pleasure"
- "Practice every kind of impurity"

Morticians render a brighter diagnosis. No wonder Scripture says, "He who hardens his heart falls into trouble" (Prov. 28:14).

A HARD HEART RUINS NOT ONLY YOUR LIFE BUT ALSO THE LIVES OF YOUR FAMILY MEMBERS.

But it gets worse. A hard heart ruins not only your life but also the lives of your family members. As an example, Jesus identified the hard heart as the wrecking ball of a marriage. When asked about divorce, Jesus said, "Moses permitted you to divorce your wives because your hearts were hard. But it was not this way from the beginning" (Matt. 19:8). When one or both people in a marriage stop trusting God to save it, they sign its death certificate. They reject the very One who can help them.

A Can-Nosed Cow

My executive assistant, Karen, saw such stubbornness in a pasture. A cow stuck her nose into a paint can and couldn't shake it off. Can-nosed cows can't breathe well, and they can't drink or eat at all. Both the cow and her calf were in a serious bovine bind.

Karen's family set out to help. But when the cow saw the rescuers coming, she set out for pasture. They pursued, but the cow escaped. They chased that cow for three days! Each time the posse drew near, the cow ran. Finally, using pickup trucks and ropes, they cornered and decanned the cow.

5 Does the story of the can-nosed cow ever represent a reality in your relationship to God? ▪ Yes ▪ No
If so, what would you say was the moral of the story?

_____

_____

Seen any can-nosed people lately? Malnourished souls? Dehydrated hearts? People who can't take a deep breath?

When billions of us imitate the cow, chaos erupts. Nations of bullheaded people ducking God and bumping into one another. We scamper, starve, and struggle. Can-nosed craziness. Isn't this the world we see? This is the world God sees.

Yet this is the world God loves. "For God so loved the world ..." This hard-hearted, stiff-necked world. We bow before gold-plated cows; still, He loves us. We stick our noses where we shouldn't; still, He pursues us. We run from the very One who can help, but He doesn't give up. He loves. He pursues. He persists. And every so often, a heart starts to soften. Let yours be one of them. Here's how.

HE DOESN'T GIVE UP.
HE LOVES.
HE PURSUES.
HE PERSISTS.

6 As you read the following instructions for softening your heart, underline the important actions you can take.

▪ Don't forget what God has done for you. Jesus once rebuked His disciples: "Are your hearts too hard to take it in? ... Don't you remember anything at all?" (Mark 8:17-18, NLT).

▪ Declare with David: "[I will] daily add praise to praise. I'll write the book on your righteousness, talk up your salvation the livelong day, never run out of good things to write or say" (Ps. 71:14-15, MSG).

▪ Catalog God's goodnesses. Meditate on them. He has fed you, led you, and earned your trust. Remember what God has done.

7 Short memories harden the heart. Make careful note of God's blessings. Take a few minutes and ask God to show you at least five ways He has blessed you in the past couple of months. Write them in the margin. Then thank God for each blessing. Be specific in your thank-Yous. Tell Him why you're grateful.

- Acknowledge what you have done against God. "If we claim we have not sinned, we are calling God a liar and showing that his word has no place in our hearts" (1 John 1:10, NLT). We all say harmful things and come up short. We fail and we forget.

NOTE: If today's discussion of sin raised memories or a painful present, consider talking privately with your small-group leader, a Christian friend, or a pastor. God loves you. Let Him.

- Confess your sins to God. Sin-hoarding stiffens us. Confession softens us.

YOUR CONVERSATION WITH GOD

As you spend time with God today, acknowledge the "golden calves" in your life and ask God to help you shatter them. Allow God to reveal reasons you have sought after illusions, false hopes, and 21st-century idols for meaning in life. Ask God to reveal not only your behavior issues but also your motives.

God and Father, I beg for simplicity. Shield me from ambition and greed. Remind me that You and You alone are my miracle worker. May my passion for You be so alive that it burns away my idols. I pray for the strength to experience absolute surrender. Save me from my self-absorbed thoughts, my selfish aspirations, my need to please, and my self-induced loneliness. Save me from all that is only me and never You.

FOR DAY 5 *turn to "The 3:16 Life" on page 136 and follow the instructions for week 2.*

GOD GAVE

Week 3

GROUP REVIEW OF WEEK 2

Follow the session plans in the leader guide on page 162.

1. Denalyn was kept off a plane because a pilot didn't receive an important message from me. Has there been a similar time in your life, when you felt that God wasn't hearing you—and didn't seem too interested in listening?

2. Describe an occasion when you have questioned the "pilot," asking God some tough life questions. How did it go? Look back at your answers to activities 2 and 3 on day 1 (pp. 30-31).

3. What attribute of God impresses you most (activities 4 and 7, day 2, pp. 34-35)? Why? On which one do you most need to focus in your praise and worship?

4. How are you growing in your realization that the God of the universe loves you so much that He is pulling for you? In what ways did you sense His doing so last week? Refer to your responses to activities 5 and 6, day 2 (p. 35).

5. Share some of your thoughts about activity 2 on page 38: What part of being tethered to God gives you comfort, and what part of the idea troubles you? What difference does God's perfect love make in your answers?

VIEW DVD MESSAGE: "GOD GAVE"

1. When we put our belief in Christ, a supernatural miracle takes place. Your heart is removed. The only perfect heart that has lived is placed within you.
2. Our _____ Heart
3. Sin is the default reaction of the human heart.

4. We need something supernatural to heal us.

5. Christ's _____ Heart

6. *Monogenes: monos*—only one + *genes*—genetic, offspring, kind

7. Everything you can say about God, you can say about Jesus.

8. A just God cannot turn a blind eye to rebellion and hard heartedness.

9. *Hyper*—in the place of or on behalf of

10. The _____ Exchange

11. Your heart and my heart were placed within Christ and punished there, so they need never be punished again.

12. Both the justice of God was satisfied, and the love of God was displayed.

Scriptures referenced: John 3:16; Jeremiah 17:9; Mark 7:21-22; Romans 3:10-11; Romans 3:23; Exodus 20:13-16; Matthew 5:28; Matthew 5:22; John 8:46; 1 Peter 2:22; Hebrews 12:14; 1 Corinthians 15:3; Galatians 1:4; Galatians 3:13; Luke 22:19-20; Isaiah 53:6; Mark 15:34; 2 Corinthians 5:17; 2 Corinthians 5:21

Message-notes blanks: (2) Unholy; (5) Holy; (10) Heart

GROUP RESPONSE

1. Why do you think we (our society) are unwilling to talk about sin?

2. What are some evidences in our world that "the heart is deceitful above all things and beyond cure" (Jer. 17:9)? What do unholy hearts look like?

3. Why would God give us His Son's heart instead of fixing our old ones?

4. From the video, what is the significance of "one and only Son"?

5. How does the story about Mayor LaGuardia illustrate both love and justice?

FOR GOD
SO LOVED
THE WORLD
THAT HE
GAVE HIS

ONE AND ONLY SON

THAT
WHOEVER
BELIEVES
IN HIM
SHALL NOT
PERISH
BUT HAVE
ETERNAL
LIFE.
JOHN 3:16

HIGHLIGHTS FOR WEEK 3

1. Every quality we attribute to God, we can attribute to Jesus.
2. Christ claims ultimate clout. Unshared supremacy. He steers the ship and pilots the plane.
3. Heaven's door has one key, and Jesus holds it.
4. Christ exchanged hearts with you.

DON'T FORGET TO WORK ON YOUR 3:16 STORY IN DAY 5.

"HE GAVE HIS ... SON"

Directions from
Christ the Redeemer

Two of our three daughters were born in the South Zone of Rio de Janeiro. We lived in the North Zone, separated from our doctor's office and hospital by a tunnel-pierced mountain range. During Denalyn's many months of pregnancy, we made the drive often.

I kept getting lost. I'm directionally challenged anyway, prone to take a wrong turn between the bedroom and bathroom. Complicate my disorientation with randomly mapped three-hundred-year-old streets, and I don't stand a chance.

I had one salvation. Jesus. Literally, Jesus. The Christ the Redeemer statue. The figure stands guard over the city, 125 feet tall with an arm span of nearly 100 feet. Perched a mile and a half above sea level on Corcovado Mountain, the elevated Jesus is always visible. As a sailor seeks land, I searched for the statue, peering between the phone lines and rooftops for the familiar face. Find Him and find my bearings.

The Christ the Redeemer statue was erected in 1931 at a cost of $250,000, most of which was privately donated by Brazilians. On July 7, 2007, the statue was named one of the New Seven Wonders of the World.[1]

1 **Describe a time you got lost or became disoriented.**
_____
_____

2 **What is it like to be lost at each of the following ages?**
as a child _____
as a teen _____
as an adult_____

3 Have you ever felt spiritually disoriented? ▪ Yes ▪ No
If so, what contributed to the disorientation?

_____

JOHN 3:16 ELEVATES
CHRIST TO THIN-AIR
LOFTINESS, CROWNING
HIM WITH THE MOST
REGAL OF TITLES: ONE
AND ONLY SON.

Like the statue in Rio, John 3:16 serves as a reliable spiritual GPS. The verse elevates Christ to thin-air loftiness, crowning Him with the most regal of titles: one and only Son.

In our session we talked about the Greek word used for *one and only*. John uses the phrase five times, in each case highlighting the unparalleled relationship between Jesus and God:

1. "The Word became flesh and made his dwelling among us. We have seen his glory, the glory of the One and Only, who came from the Father, full of grace and truth" (John 1:14).

2. "No one has ever seen God, but God the One and Only, who is at the Father's side, has made him known" (John 1:18).

3. "For God so loved the world that he gave his one and only Son" (John 3:16).

4. "Whoever believes in him is not condemned, but whoever does not believe stands condemned already because he has not believed in the name of God's one and only Son" (John 3:18).

5. "This is how God showed his love among us: He sent his one and only Son into the world that we might live through him" (1 John 4:9).

4 Based on the Scriptures above, match the verse references with the roles Jesus plays as the One and Only. Write a letter beside each number.

___ 1. John 1:14   a. God-revealer

___ 2. John 1:18   b. Judge

___ 3. John 3:16   c. God Almighty

___ 4. John 3:18   d. Gift

___ 5. 1 John 4:9   e. Glory-bearer

                              f. Love-demonstration

Monogenes highlights the particular relationship between Jesus and God. Though God is the Father of all humanity, Jesus alone is the monogenetic Son of God, because only Christ has God's genes. Only Christ is God by nature. The familiar translation "only begotten Son" (John 3:16, NASB) conveys this truth. When parents beget or conceive a child, they transfer their DNA to the newborn. Jesus shares God's DNA. Jesus isn't begotten in the sense that He began but in the sense that He and God have the same essence, eternal life span, unending wisdom, and tireless energy. Every quality we attribute to God, we can attribute to Jesus.

"Anyone who has seen me has seen the Father!" Jesus claimed (John 14:9, NLT). And the Epistle to the Hebrews concurs: "[Christ] is the radiance of [God's] glory and the exact representation of His nature" (1:3, NASB).

5 **Why do you think it's important to realize that Jesus shares God's DNA?**

_____

_____

How does that realization impact the way you interact with Jesus?

_____

Jesus claims not the most authority but all authority: "My Father has entrusted everything to me. No one truly knows the Son except the Father, and no one truly knows the Father except the Son and those to whom the Son chooses to reveal him" (Matt. 11:27, NLT).

Don't hurry through those words. They're either the last straw or the ultimate truth. They warrant deliberate thought.

Christ claims ultimate clout. Unshared supremacy. He is to history what a weaver is to a tapestry. " 'My thoughts are nothing like your thoughts,' says the LORD. 'And my ways are far beyond

(#4 answers: 1-e; 2-a; 3-d; 4-b; 5-f)

ONLY CHRIST HAS GOD'S GENES. …
EVERY QUALITY WE ATTRIBUTE TO GOD, WE CAN ATTRIBUTE TO JESUS.

MATTHEW 28:18, NASB

"All authority has been given to Me in heaven and on earth."

AS IF GOD SAYS, "MY ARTISTRY IS FAR BEYOND ANYTHING YOU COULD IMAGINE."

anything you could imagine'" (Isa. 55:8, NLT). A root meaning of the word translated *thoughts* is skillful craftsmanship. As if God says, "My artistry is far beyond anything you could imagine."

6 **What does it mean to recognize Christ's supremacy or authority in your life?**

_____

_____

Is there any specific area in your life where you are not recognizing His authority?

_____

_____

YOUR CONVERSATION WITH GOD

Take a moment to access God's GPS. Are you having difficulty finding your way through the detours and potholes of the day-to-day? Ask God to accompany you as you take an inventory of your direction. Do you look to Jesus for more than a periodic bailout? Is He your North Star, guiding you to your ultimate destination? Are you willing to go where He is calling you to go today?

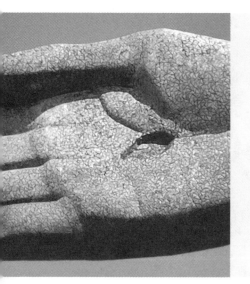

Lord Jesus, My light and my salvation, I struggle daily with directions, and when I, like a stubborn, closed-fisted child, refuse to follow You, I am without hope. No map, compass, or voice from the dashboard can lead me as You can. I can go fast. That's what this world demands of me. I've made an art of going nowhere fast! I'm through with harried agendas and the hairpin turns of emotion. I just need You, Jesus. You are enough to see me home.

"ONE AND ONLY SON"

The One and Only Revealer

Christ: the one and only Ruler who claims to be the one and only Revealer: "No one truly knows the Son except the Father, and no one truly knows the Father except the Son" (Matt. 11:27, NLT).

Jesus enjoys an intimacy with God, a mutuality the Father shares with no one else. Jesus "exists at the very heart of the Father" and "has made him plain as day" (John 1:18, MSG).

When Jesus says, "In My Father's house are many mansions" (John 14:2, NKJV), count on it. He knows. He has walked them. When Christ declares, "Your Father knows what you need before you ask Him" (Matt. 6:8, NASB), believe it. After all, "He was in the beginning with God" (John 1:2, NASB).

> JESUS ENJOYS AN INTIMACY WITH GOD, A MUTUALITY THE FATHER SHARES WITH NO ONE ELSE.

1 **What do you need Jesus to reveal to you about the Father? Be as specific as possible.**

_____

_____

_____

_____

_____

2 **Pause to pray. Look back at the roles of Christ in day 1, activity 4 (p. 54). Appeal to the Son on the basis of those roles to show you the Father's heart about the concerns you identified above.**

Jesus claims to be not a top theologian, an accomplished theologian, or even the Supreme Theologian but rather the only Theologian. "No one truly knows the Father except the Son." He does not say, "No one truly knows the Father like the Son" or "in the fashion of the Son." Rather, "No one truly knows the Father except the Son."

HEAVEN'S DOOR HAS ONE KEY, AND JESUS HOLDS IT.

Heaven's door has one key, and Jesus holds it. He knows the dimensions of God's throne room, the fragrance of its incense, the favorite songs of the unceasing choir. He has a unique, one-of-a-kind, unrivaled knowledge of God and wants to share His knowledge with you: "No one truly knows the Father except the Son and those to whom the Son chooses to reveal him" (Matt. 11:27, NLT).

3 **Circle all the words that describe your response to the idea that Jesus knows God intimately and completely.**

- Assurance
- Excitement
- Skepticism
- Confidence
- Boldness

- Joy
- Laughter
- Tears
- Fear
- Peace

- Motivation
- Confusion
- Adoration
- Awe
- Other: _____

JESUS DOESN'T BOAST IN HIS KNOWLEDGE; HE SHARES IT. HE DOESN'T GLOAT; HE GIVES.

Jesus doesn't boast in His knowledge; He shares it. He doesn't gloat; He gives. He doesn't revel; He reveals. He reveals to us the secrets of eternity. And He shares them not just with the top brass or purebred but with the hungry and needy. In the very next line Jesus invites: "Come to me, all of you who are weary and carry heavy burdens, and I will give you rest. Take my yoke upon you. Let me teach you, because I am humble and gentle at heart, and you will find rest for your souls" (Matt. 11:28-29, NLT).

Do yourself a favor. Find the brightest highlighter manufactured and the darkest ink produced. Underscore, underline, and accept His invitation: "Let Me teach you …"

One of my Boy Scout assignments was to build a kite. One of my blessings as a Boy Scout was a kite-building dad. He built a lot of things: scooters on skates, go-karts. Why, he even built our house. A kite to him was stick figures to Van Gogh. Could handle them in his sleep.

With wood glue, poles, and newspaper we fashioned a sky-dancing masterpiece: red, white, and blue and shaped like a box. We launched our creation on the back of a March wind. But after some minutes my kite caught a downdraft and plunged. I tightened the string, raced in reverse, and did all I could to maintain elevation. But it was too late. She Hindenburged earthward.

Envision a redheaded, heartsick 12-year-old standing over his collapsed kite. That was me. Envision a square-bodied man with ruddy skin and coveralls, placing his hand on the boy's shoulder. That was my kite-making dad. He surveyed the heap of sticks and paper and assured, "It's OK. We can fix this." I believed him. Why not? He spoke with authority.

4 **What are you facing that requires God's hand on your shoulder and His reassurance "It's OK; we can fix this"?**

_____

_____

To all whose lives feel like a crashed kite, Jesus says with authority, "We can fix this. Let Me teach you. Let Me teach you how to handle your money, long Mondays, and cranky in-laws. Let Me teach you why people fight, death comes, and forgiveness counts. But most of all, let Me teach you why on earth you are on this earth."

5 **What are some things you wish Jesus would teach you?**

_____

_____

_____

My Kite-Building Dad

TO ALL WHOSE LIVES FEEL LIKE A CRASHED KITE, HE SAYS, "WE CAN FIX THIS. LET ME TEACH YOU."

6 **What do you need to be reminded of that He has already taught you and positively changed your life?**

_____

_____

Don't we need to learn? We know so much, and yet we know so little. The age of information is the age of confusion: much know-how, hardly any know-why. We need answers. Jesus offers them.

But can we trust Him? Only one way to know. Do what I did in Rio. Seek Him out. Lift up your eyes and set your sights on Jesus. No passing glances or occasional glimpses. Enroll in His school. "Let Me teach you …" Make Him your polestar, your point of reference. Search the crowded streets and shadow-casting roofs until you spot His face and then set your sights on Him.

You'll find more than a hospital.

You'll find the One and Only.

YOUR CONVERSATION WITH GOD

Perhaps you are like almost everyone around you, broken and messy, seeking fixes and solutions and wondering, _How did I get this way?_ If that's you, what puzzles you endlessly as you try to look and act presentable before the neighbors?

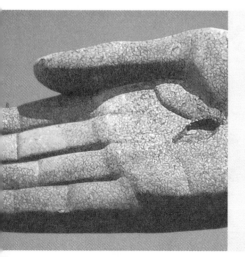

Lord Jesus, I realize that I can't be fixed as easily as a kite or a carburetor. The world is awash with quick fixes and flimsy, glossed-over repair manuals. I don't need more knowledge, more money, or more acceptance from people. I need a Savior who can put it all back together. I'm amazed that You accept me in my brokenness, but I know that You want me to experience life beyond my barely-getting-by existence. Fix me, Jesus.

OUR HEART PROBLEM

Irregular Heartbeat

In our session I told you about my episode with a heart condition. I still can't get excited about having the "best kind of cardiac concern." But I sure get excited about my other Cardiologist—the one who trades broken, diseased, sin-stained hearts for His perfect, clean, pure heart.

Where do you find such a physician? You can reach Him at this number—3:16. At the heart of this verse, He deals with the heart of our problem: "For God so loved the world that he gave his one and only Son."

Possibly the most amazing part came in how Jesus exchanges our bad hearts for His good one. We find the description all over the pages of the New Testament.

1 **Read Peter's explanation below. Then explain it in your own words.**

"²²*He 'did not commit sin,*
*   and no deceit was found in His mouth';*
²³*when reviled, He did not revile in return;*
*   when suffering, He did not threaten,*
*   but committed Himself to the One who judges justly.*
²⁴*He Himself bore our sins*
*   in His body on the tree,*
*   so that, having died to sins,*
*   we might live for righteousness;*
*   by 'His wounding you have been healed.'"*
1 Peter 2:22-24, HCSB

2 Explain Peter's words. I've given you some hints to help you get started.

a. What made Jesus uniquely qualified for the job (v. 22)?

_____

_____

b. How did He conduct Himself on the cross (v. 23)?

_____

_____

c. What results did Jesus accomplish (v. 24)?

_____

_____

_____

THE TROUBLE IS MANY, MAYBE MOST, PEOPLE IN OUR DAY DON'T EVEN SEE THE NEED FOR A NEW HEART. THEY DON'T SEEK TREATMENT BECAUSE THEY HAVE BECOME BLIND TO THE DISEASE.

The trouble is many, maybe most, people in our day don't even see the need for a new heart. They don't seek treatment because they have become blind to the disease. Like the man on the airplane, they think they're doing OK. He thought the idea of Jesus' dying in his place was ridiculous because he didn't think he had a sin problem.

3 From the following pair of statements, check the one you think better explains to the man who didn't think he was a sinner why he needs the gift of God's Son.

◼ a. Through the circumstances of life, you could lose your job, your reputation, and your family; only the gift of God's Son is certain.

◼ b. There's more to life than present, temporary circumstances; the gift of God's Son ensures eternal life that goes beyond good or bad present circumstances.

4 Explain why you consider the answer you chose the better response. _____

_____

_____

_____

This generation is oddly silent about sin. Some mental-health professionals mock our need for divine forgiveness. Because they believe in the natural goodness of human nature, some actually believe that teaching people about sin causes mental, spiritual, and behavioral problems. For a good discussion of this view, see the LifeWay resource *How Now Shall We Live?*[2]

5 Which of these statements do you think best explains why our generation is oddly silent about sin? Check one.

a. We're the therapeutic generation that explains bad behavior in terms of illnesses and addictions.

b. We've been taught to assume everyone is basically good.

c. We don't want anyone to feel guilty or criticized.

d. We reject God, so there's no one to hold us accountable to an absolute moral standard.

Why did you select this explanation of our generation's silence about sin? _____

_____

_____

Isn't it amazing? We live in a day when people ignore our own sin and disregard or even look down on God the Son. Blind to the reality of the evil that inhabits our world and our lives, we act as if we are sufficient on our own merits.

Our self-sufficient boasting reminds me of an experience when I met golf legend Byron Nelson. Brand-new to the game, I had

Golf Legend
Byron Nelson

just broken a hundred on the golf course for the first time. A friend had an appointment with Mr. Nelson and asked me to come along. En route I bragged about my double-digit score, offering a hole-by-hole summary. Fearing I might do the same with the retired icon, my friend asked what I knew of Byron Nelson's accomplishments, and then he told me:

- Five major titles
- Eleven consecutive victories
- An average score of 69 during the streak

My score of ninety-eight seemed suddenly insignificant. Mr. Nelson's standard silenced me. Jesus' perfection silences us.

YOUR CONVERSATION WITH GOD

How's your heart? Filled with joy over new life? Stained by habitual sin? Has it been victimized by people? Does it race with anxiety when you think about your family? Or maybe it's just hard because you've offered it so many times to others and experienced shame or rejection. How's your heart?

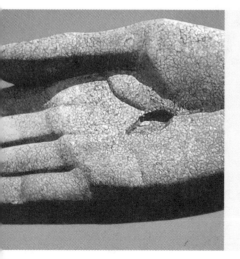

My Jesus who committed no sin, thank You for giving me a new spiritual heart. I want to take hold of it. I need You to remind me daily that the work has already been done. You carried the cross—my punishment—and You will not carry it again. It's done. I need You to help me settle this truth deep in my bones. I don't have to muddle through life with a sense of spiritual inferiority, because You transfused new life into my soul. Thank You for what You did on the cross for me.

THE HEART SWAP

How does God respond to our unholy hearts? Can a good cardiologist spot irregularity and dismiss it? Can God overlook our sins as innocent mistakes? No. He is the one and only Judge. He issues decrees, not opinions; commands, not suggestions. They are truth. They emerge from His holy self. Violate them, and you dethrone Him—dethrone Him at the highest cost.

Jesus made His position clear: "Anyone whose life is not holy will never see the Lord" (Heb. 12:14, NCV). Hard-hearted souls will not populate heaven.

So where does that leave us? It leaves us drawing hope from a five-letter Greek word. *Hyper* means "for the sake of" or "on behalf of."[3] New Testament writers repeatedly turned to this preposition to describe the work of Christ:

- "Christ died for *[hyper]* our sins" (1 Cor. 15:3).
- "Jesus gave himself for *[hyper]* our sins" (Gal. 1:4, NCV).
- "Christ redeemed us from the curse of the Law, having become a curse for *[hyper]* us" (Gal. 3:13, NASB).
- Jesus Himself prophesied: "The good shepherd lays down his life for *[hyper]* the sheep" (John 10:11).
- "Greater love has no one than this, that he lay down his life for *[hyper]* his friends" (John 15:13).
- Before His death Jesus took bread and explained, "This is my body given for *[hyper]* you" (Luke 22:19). And presenting the cup, he explained: "This cup is the new covenant in my blood, which is poured out for *[hyper]* you" (v. 20).

HEBREWS 12:14, NCV

"Anyone whose life

is not holy will never

see the Lord."

HYPER

Greek word meaning "for,"
"for the sake of," or "on behalf of"

1 In your life experience has anyone ever put himself or herself on the line for you? ▪ Yes ▪ No If so, would you describe it?

_____

_____

If you thought of an instance, you probably had no trouble recalling your feelings toward the person. A friend named Beth gave one of her kidneys to a stranger—a significant gift, but she didn't receive the diseased kidney back in her body. Contrast that with the self-sacrifice of the perfect Creator's giving Himself.

2 Read the words below and check three that you think best characterize Jesus' willingness to lay down His life on your behalf or in your place.

▪ Breathtaking ▪ Courageous ▪ Substitutionary

▪ Merciful ▪ Infinite ▪ Compassionate

▪ Sacrificial ▪ Awesome ▪ Divine

▪ Manly ▪ Judicial ▪ Excruciating

ISAIAH 53:6, HCSB

"We all went astray

like sheep;

we all have turned

to our own way;

and the LORD has

punished Him

for the iniquity of us all."

3 Why did you choose those answers?

_____

_____

The point is crucial. Christ exchanged hearts with you. He placed your sin in Himself and invited God to punish it. See Isaiah 53:6 in the margin.

4 Insert your name in the blanks in 2 Corinthians 5:21 and read the verse aloud.

_"God made [Jesus] who had no sin to be sin for _____, so that in him _____ might become the righteousness of God."_

5 As you heard these words aloud, how did they affect you? Or how do you think they should affect you?

_____

_____

A SWAP, NOT A TRANSPLANT

Though healthy, Jesus took our disease on Himself. Though diseased, we who accept His offer are pronounced healthy. More than pardoned, we are declared innocent. We enter heaven not with healed hearts but with His heart. It is as if we have never sinned. Slowly read the announcement of Paul: "If anyone is in Christ, he is a new creation; the old has gone, the new has come!" (2 Cor. 5:17).

This is no transplant, mind you, but a swap. The holy and the vile exchange locations. God makes healthy what was sick, right what was wrong, straight what was crooked.

Steven Vryhof witnessed the impact of this gift in a Lutheran church on the coast of Sweden. A handful of the faithful had gathered to sing, pray, and celebrate communion. He took his turn at the altar, received the bread and the wine, and returned to his seat.

As the minister turned his back to the congregation and began putting away the elements, two more worshipers came forward. A middle-aged woman pushed her mother in a wheelchair. "The mother," writes Vryhof, "had the classic nursing-home look: slumped to the right, thin, scraggly, colorless hair, vacant eyes, and a slack-jaw with her tongue showing a bit. She was here for communion."

Everyone but the minister knew of the two women at the altar. When he finally realized their presence, he retrieved the elements and administered the piece of bread and the sip of wine. He then paused, looked the old woman directly in the eye, and declared the customary blessing: "Our Lord Jesus Christ, whose body and blood you have received, preserve your soul unto everlasting life."

The irony struck Vryhof. The woman was too old to keep her balance or her head straight. She brought nothing but a bent body

WE ENTER HEAVEN NOT WITH HEALED HEARTS BUT WITH HIS HEART.

A Special Communion

and feeble bones. Dare one believe that heaven cares for such a soul? The moment Vryhof asked the question, the church bells erupted, pealing, ringing unexpectedly and majestically. It was as if God Himself were declaring, "I will claim the frail, preserve the weak, and secure the weary. Let them come."[4]

And so we do. Scarred and journey-hardened, we come. "Can You do something with this heart?" we ask.

He nods and smiles. "Suppose we discuss a swap."

YOUR CONVERSATION WITH GOD

Reflect on the things that you bring to the table to help God. Now reflect on the absurdity of that statement. This week we've walked through truths that underscore the fact that God doesn't need what we bring to Him, but we certainly need what He brings to us. That's the root of unconditional love: Nothing in our hands, and yet He loves us still. He just loves us.

Lord, I get it. **YOU LOVE ME.** *Seeing everything—every shortcut, every stumbling step, every day I am stuck in the mire of self-doubt and worry.* **YOU LOVE ME.** *And there's nothing I can do that will change Your love. Not illness, rebellion, self-induced loneliness, or even my questions. Nothing!* **YOU LOVE ME.** *Though I long to earn Your love, even then, Your love marches on! Even when I fail,* **YOU LOVE ME.** *Jesus, I realize that You didn't die to make me better. You died because* **YOU LOVE ME.** *And Your love is enough. Yes, it's enough to carry me. It is enough to redeem me. Not salvation by me. Salvation for me. Because* **YOU LOVE ME.**

FOR DAY 5 *turn to "The 3:16 Life" on page 140 and follow the instructions for week 3.*

WE BELIEVE

Week 4

GROUP REVIEW OF WEEK 3

Follow the session plans in the leader guide on page 164.

1. What are some things you wish Jesus, the one and only Revealer, would teach you? Share some things He has already taught you, positively changing your life as a result (day 2, activities 5 and 6, pp. 59–60).

2. From your responses to activity 5 on day 3 (p. 63), what are some reasons you think our generation is oddly silent about sin? What is an appropriate Christian response?

3. How does Jesus put Himself on the line for you? How do you tend to respond to His great gift (see day 4, activities 1–3, p. 66)?

4. In the spiritual rather than the medical sense, what are important distinctions between a heart transplant and a heart swap (see pp. 67–68)?

5. In your opinion, how important to your complete 3:16 story is the part about what Jesus has done for you? Why?

VIEW DVD MESSAGE: "WE BELIEVE"

1. God wants you to depend entirely on the strength of Christ.
2. You can't _____ you.
3. "To the one who does not work but believes in Him who justifies the ungodly, his faith is [credited] as righteousness" (Rom. 4:5, ESV).

4. "I give them eternal life, and they shall never perish; no one can snatch them out of my hand" (John 10:28).

5. When you become a child of God, you stay a child of God.

6. A soul that is sealed by God is safe.

7. If you are in Christ, He will never let you go.

8. You're not going to surprise Him with your mistakes.

9. Only Christ guarantees a safe landing.

10. Because His grip is stronger than your slip, you will not fall.

11. Don't believe in them. They can't _____ you.

Scriptures referenced: John 3:16; Romans 4:5; John 10:28;
John 1:12; Ephesians 1:13; John 14:6; Acts 4:12; 1 Corinthians 8:4
Message-notes blanks: (2) save; (11) save

GROUP RESPONSE

1. How does this claim of Christ run counter to our culture of tolerance?

2. How did the Team Hoyt story affect you? How does it illustrate dependence on Christ?

3. What are some of the things people mistakenly trust in to save themselves?

4. How should confidence that God will not let go of you affect your daily life?

5. What would you say is the crucial difference between Christianity and other world religions? Why is this so important?

6. What was the most meaningful or encouraging statement you heard is this session and why?

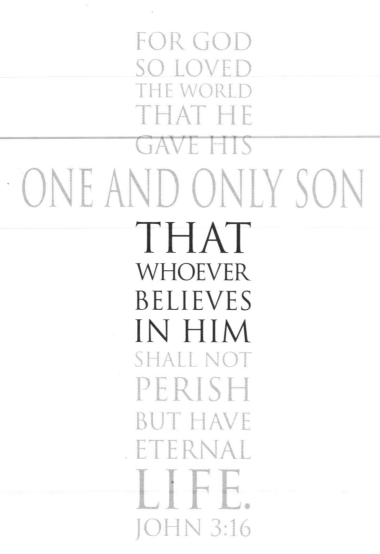

FOR GOD
SO LOVED
THE WORLD
THAT HE
GAVE HIS
ONE AND ONLY SON
THAT
WHOEVER
BELIEVES
IN HIM
SHALL NOT
PERISH
BUT HAVE
ETERNAL
LIFE.
JOHN 3:16

HIGHLIGHTS FOR WEEK 4

1. Belief in Jesus involves an action of faith, not simply an acknowledgment of fact.
2. God works, and we trust.
3. Jesus says, "My death on the cross saves you."
4. A soul sealed by God is safe because God's grip is stronger than your slip.

DON'T FORGET TO WORK ON YOUR 3:16 STORY IN DAY 5.

"THAT WHOEVER BELIEVES"

"Tell me my part again," I groaned.

"Just trust me," she assured. *She* was a bubbly, college-aged, baseball-capped rope holder. *Trust me* translated into a backward leap off a 50-foot cliff, wearing a belay harness and a what-did-I-get-myself-into expression.

Some people love rappelling. They relish the stomach-in-the-throat sensation. Not me. I prefer the seat-in-the-chair one. I had traveled to Colorado to experience a week of rest to the fullest. Fresh air, great views. Good coffee, long talks. These events made my list. Half gainers off the mountain didn't.

Blame persuasive friends and stupid pride for my presence on the peak. The platform team assured me of a safe landing.

"Ever done this?" the girl asked.

"No."

She handed me a leather harness and told me to step in. "It's kind of like a diaper." She smiled, all too chipper. *I may need a diaper,* I thought.

"What about you?" I inquired. "Have you lowered anyone down the mountain?"

"Been working here all summer." She beamed.

It was barely July.

"It's simple," she continued as she clipped me. "Hold the rope and jump. Bounce off the wall with your feet."

Someone should make a law: the words *jump, bounce,* and *wall* should never be spoken in the same breath.

A 50-Foot Cliff

"How do I keep from crashing?"

"You don't. I do that."

"You?"

"Yes, I hold your rope." Little comfort. Not only was she half my age, she was also half my size—more the ballet than the belay sort.

"But don't I do something?" I begged.

"YOU TRUST ME."

"You trust me."

1 Have you ever been in a situation in which you trusted someone with your safety or your life? ▪ Yes ▪ No
If so, was this a struggle for you? Why or why not?

_____

2 What minimal conditions or characteristics must a person have to be considered trustworthy?

_____

_____

I inched up to the edge of the cliff and looked down. Frodo felt safer looking into the pit.

"Do you have any valuables?" I heard a voice ask.

"Only my life."

"You're funny," she chirped, sounding so much like my daughters that I remembered my will was out-of-date. "Come on. It's your turn!"

I gave her one more look. A look akin to the one the 3:16 promise often prompts. Can I really trust that "whoever believes in him shall not perish"?

The girl told me to fix my gaze on her. As I took the plunge, she shouted, "Keep your eyes up here!" I didn't have to be told twice. Of the two of us, she was the only one smiling.

But because she did her work, I landed safely. Next trip, however, you'll find me in a chair on the porch.

3 James 2:19 tells us that even demons have a form of belief. How do action, trust, and faith combine to express belief?

_____

_____

_____

_____

JAMES 2:19

"You believe that there is one God. Good! Even the demons believe that—and shudder."

4 Is Jesus trustworthy? The Bible says, "Yes!" Match the verses below with the reasons listed in the margin. Write the corresponding letter beside the number.

___ 1. "Jesus … said, 'All authority in heaven and on earth has been given to me'" (Matt. 28:18).

___ 2. "Jesus Christ is the same yesterday and today and forever" (Heb. 13:8).

___ 3. "I and the Father are one" (John 10:30).

___ 4. "This is how we know what love is: Jesus Christ laid down his life for us" (1 John 3:16).

a. Jesus loves us so much that He died for us.

b. Jesus has all power and authority.

c. Jesus never changes.

d. Jesus is God.

(#4 answers: 1-b; 2-c; 3-d; 4-a)

YOUR CONVERSATION WITH GOD

Reflect on the nature of true belief. Ask God to reveal those parts of your life that wrestle with moments of disbelief, doubt, and concern. What is God telling you through this study?

Jesus, invisible companion, I confess that many times I struggle with things I can't see or touch. Often my first thoughts of faith in my work, my finances, and my family are fearful and hesitant. Lord, banish my desire to stay in my comfort zone. I know You desire me to trust in, cling to, rely on You. You've called me to live a dangerous, holy adventure for Your glory! I will fall toward You today, Jesus.

"In Him"

A Simple Invitation

Jesus' invitation seems too simple. We gravitate to other verbs. *Work* has a better ring to it: "Whoever works for Him will be saved." *Satisfy* fits nicely: "Whoever satisfies Him will be saved." But *believe?* Shouldn't I do more?

This seems to be the struggle of Nicodemus. It was his conversation with Christ, remember, that set the stage for John 3:16. Jesus' "You must be born again" command struck the scholar—and some of us—the way the words of the take-a-leap girl struck me as I stood on the edge of the cliff. What's my part?

1 **Is it easier for you to *believe* or to *work?* Why?**

_____

_____

SALVATION IS EQUALLY SIMPLE. GOD WORKS, AND WE TRUST.

The baby takes a passive role in the birthing process. Salvation is equally simple. God works, and we trust. Such a thought troubled Nicodemus. There must be more. Jesus comforted the visiting professor with an account from the Torah, Nicodemus's favorite book: "As Moses lifted up the bronze snake on a pole in the wilderness, so the Son of Man must be lifted up, so that everyone who believes in him will have eternal life" (John 3:14-15, NLT).

Nicodemus knew this event. A one-sentence reference was enough for him to understand. To us, however, the verse is cryptic.

Why did Jesus precede the 3:16 offer with a reference to a serpent in the wilderness? Here is the backstory.

The wandering Israelites were grumbling at Moses again. Though camped on the border of the promised land and beneficiaries of four decades of God's provisions, the Hebrews sounded off like spoiled trust-fund brats: "Why have you brought us up out of Egypt to die in the wilderness?" (Num. 21:5, NKJV).

God had had all the moaning he could take. "So the LORD sent fiery serpents among the people, and they bit the people; and many of the people of Israel died" (v. 6, NKJV).

Survivors begged Moses to plead with God for mercy: "'We have sinned. ... Pray to the LORD that He take away the serpents from us.' So Moses prayed for the people" (v. 7, NKJV).

"Then the LORD said to Moses, 'Make a fiery serpent, and set it on a pole; and it shall be that everyone who is bitten, when he looks at it, shall live.' So Moses made a bronze serpent, and put it on a pole; and so it was, if a serpent had bitten anyone, when he looked at the bronze serpent, he lived" (vv. 8-9, NKJV).

This passage was a solemn prophecy. And it was also a simple promise. Snake-bit Israelites found healing by looking at the pole. Sinners will find healing by looking to Christ: "Everyone who believes in him will have eternal life" (John 3:15, NLT).

2 **Why do you think Jesus used the story of the snake on the pole to clear up confusion about faith and works? What does the story tell you?**

_____

_____

3 **Underline the words or phrases in the following verses that tell God's way to eternal life.**

   a. *"Whoever believes in the Son has eternal life, but whoever rejects the Son will not see life."* John 3:36

3:16

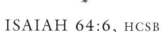

ROMANS 10:9

"If you confess with your mouth, 'Jesus is Lord,' and believe in your heart that God raised him from the dead, you will be saved."

ISAIAH 64:6, HCSB

"All of us have become like something unclean, and all our righteous acts are like a polluted garment."

b. *"Whoever hears my word and believes him who sent me has eternal life and will not be condemned."* John 5:24

c. *"These are written that you may believe that Jesus is the Christ, the Son of God, and that by believing you may have life in his name."* John 20:31

d. *"If you confess with your mouth, 'Jesus is Lord,' and believe in your heart that God raised him from the dead, you will be saved."* Romans 10:9

A SIMPLE PROCESS

The simplicity troubles many people. We expect a more complicated cure, a more elaborate treatment. Moses and his followers might have expected more as well. Manufacture an ointment. Invent a therapeutic lotion. Treat one another. Or at least fight back. Break out the sticks and stones and attack the snakes.

We too expect a more proactive assignment, to have to conjure up a remedy for our sin. Some mercy seekers have donned hair shirts, climbed cathedral steps on their knees, or traversed hot rocks on bare feet.

Others of us have written our own Bible verse: "God helps those who help themselves" (Popular Opinion 1:1). We'll fix ourselves, thank you. We'll make up for our mistakes with contributions, our guilt with busyness. We'll overcome failures with hard work. We'll find salvation the old-fashioned way: we'll earn it.

4 **What does Isaiah 64:6 (margin) imply that we bring to the table?**

_____

5 **As you read the following Scripture passage from Paul's letter to the Philippians, underline the things in which Paul might have placed his confidence for salvation. I've underlined one for you.**

78

*"We rely on what Christ Jesus has done for us. We put no
confidence in human effort, though I could have confidence
in my own effort if anyone could. Indeed, if others have reason
for confidence in their own efforts, I have even more!*

    *"I was circumcised when I was eight days old. I am a
<u>pure-blooded citizen of Israel</u> and a member of the tribe of
Benjamin—a real Hebrew if there ever was one! I was a
member of the Pharisees, who demand the strictest obedience
to the Jewish law. I was so zealous that I harshly persecuted
the church. And as for righteousness, I obeyed the law without
fault."* Philippians 3:3-6, NLT

6   **How do you think the church emphasizes *doing* vs.
believing today? Make a list of ways we're tempted
to try to enhance our position with God.**

_____

_____

7   **Continue reading, and underline the words describing
the way Paul became right with God.**

*"I once thought these things were valuable, but now I consider
them worthless because of what Christ has done. … I no longer
count on my own righteousness through obeying the law; rather,
I become righteous through faith in Christ. For God's way of
making us right with himself depends on faith."*
Philippians 3:3-7,9, NLT

8   **In the margin write a summary statement in your own
words describing what is *not* enough to make you right
with God and what *is* required. If you choose, you may
write a song lyric or poem.**

Christ says to us what the rope-holding girl said to me: "Your part is to trust. Trust me to do what you can't."

Jesus invites you to do the same with Him. Trust Him to do a work you cannot accomplish by your own efforts, strength, or worth. But just Him. Not Moses or any other leader. Not other snake-bitten souls. Not even you. You can't fix you.

9 Which of the following can make you right with God and result in eternal life? Check all that apply.

- a. Trust in and follow the teachings of great religious leaders like Mohammed, Buddha, or the Dalai Lama.
- b. Keep track so my good deeds outweigh my bad.
- c. Look to Jesus and believe Him and His work on my behalf.
- d. Join a church, work hard, attend regularly, and give.
- e. Do my best to follow the church's list of do's and don'ts.

(#9 answer: c)

Jesus said, "My Father's will is that everyone who looks to the Son and believes in Him shall have eternal life" (John 6:40). Look to Jesus … and believe!

YOUR CONVERSATION WITH GOD

Take an inventory of self-saving actions, emotions, and thoughts. Ask God, "Am I serving You because I love You or am I serving because I want to add to my assurance of salvation?" The "adding to" could become the sin of idolatry, when we put our works as savior equal to or above the sacrificial gift of Christ's sacrifice.

Father, I confess my sins of self-salvation. I repent of the desire to take credit for anything good that finds its source in me. Reveal to me the good news that even though my works are filthy rags, they are made perfect through the cleansing power of Your Son. I'm so thankful that I'm not signing up for a perfection club. I don't have the resources to pay the dues. But hallelujah! You do!

ONE WAY ONLY

The phrase "believes in him" doesn't digest well in our day of self-sufficient spiritual food. "Believe in yourself" is the common menu selection of our day. Try harder. Work longer. Dig deeper. Self-reliance is our goal.

And tolerance is our virtue. "In him" smacks of exclusion. Don't all paths lead to heaven? Islam, Hinduism, Buddhism, and humanism? Salvation comes in many forms, right? Christ walks upriver on this topic. Salvation is found not in self or in them but in Him.

Don't believe in you; you can't save you. And don't believe in others; they can't save you.

YOU CAN'T SAVE YOU!

Christ's followers refused to soften or shift the spotlight. Peter announced, "There is salvation in no one else! God has given no other name under heaven by which we must be saved" (Acts 4:12, NLT).

1 **Do you believe truth is exclusive? Answer the following math problem: 8 + 8 = ___**
 ▪ a. 15   ▪ b. 16.2   ▪ c. 16   ▪ d. 64

2 **Who was the first president of the United States?**
 ▪ a. Abraham Lincoln
 ▪ b. Ringo Starr
 ▪ c. John Quincy Adams
 ▪ d. George Washington

3 **Red mixed with yellow gives you which color?**
 ▪ a. Orange   ▪ b. Purple
 ▪ c. Green   ▪ d. Blue

4 We know there's only one answer to each question. Why do you think some struggle with the exclusivity of Jesus?

_____

_____

JOHN 14:6, RSV

"I am the way, and the truth, and the life; no one comes to the Father, but by me."

■

ACTS 4:12, NLT

"There is salvation in no one else! God has given no other name under heaven by which we must be saved."

In areas like these, truth is absolute. Only one answer is correct. Many recoil at such definitiveness. John 14:6 and Acts 4:12 sound primitive in this era of broadband and broad minds. The world is shrinking, cultures are blending, borders are bending; this is the day of inclusion. All roads lead to heaven, right?

But can they? The sentence makes good talk-show fodder, but is it accurate? Can all approaches to God be correct?

5 The Bible leaves no doubt about the exclusivity of Christ, period. What does Jesus say about Himself in John 14:6 and Peter echo in Acts 4:12?

_____

6 Think of someone you know who has chosen not to believe in the exclusivity of Jesus. Write the person's initials here: _____

Why do you think this person struggles with embracing Jesus as the only way to God?

_____

_____

Pause to pray that God's Spirit will open that person's understanding to believe the truth about Jesus. Begin thinking of opportunities you might have to share these truths with this person. Write notes in the margin.

How can all religions lead to God when they are so different? We don't tolerate such illogic in other matters. We don't pretend that all roads lead to London or all ships sail to Australia. In our session together we had fun with the idea that all flights land in Rome. The idea is comical because we know every flight does not go to Rome.

Every path does not lead to God. Jesus blazed a stand-alone trail void of self-salvation. He cleared a one-of-a-kind passageway uncluttered by human effort. Christ came not for the strong but for the weak, not for the righteous but for the sinner. We enter His way on confession of our need, not completion of our deeds. He offers a unique-to-Him invitation in which He works and we trust, He dies and we live, He invites and we believe.

7 **What does 1 John 5:11-12 say, and what's at stake?**

_____

_____

8 **Circle the responses in the following verses that illustrate the rejection of eternal life.**

1. *"Even after Jesus had done all these miraculous signs in their presence, they still would not believe in him."* John 12:37
2. *"At Iconium Paul and Barnabas went as usual into the Jewish synagogue. There they spoke so effectively that a great number of Jews and Gentiles believed. But the Jews who refused to believe stirred up the Gentiles."* Acts 14:1-2
3. *"Some of them became obstinate; they refused to believe."* Acts 19:9
4. *"Some were convinced by what he said; but others would not believe."* Acts 28:24

What was the common response of rejection?

_____

HE WORKS
AND WE TRUST.

∎

HE DIES
AND WE LIVE.

∎

HE INVITES
AND WE BELIEVE.

1 JOHN 5:11-12

"God has given us eternal life, and this life is in his Son. He who has the Son has life; he who does not have the Son of God does not have life."

83

We have a choice just like them. We can refuse to believe, or we believe in him: "The work God wants you to do is this: Believe the One he sent" (John 6:29, NCV).

Believe in yourself? No. Believe in Him.

Believe in them? No. Believe in Him.

And those who do, those who believe "in him shall not perish but have eternal life" (John 3:16).

JOHN 3:18, HCSB

"Anyone who believes in Him is not judged, but anyone who does not believe is already judged, because he has not believed in the name of the One and Only Son of God."

YOUR CONVERSATION WITH GOD

Think of the people you've encountered over the past few months who are counting on other things besides Jesus to bring salvation to their eternal future. They might be people of other religions or perspectives. They may be people that you know personally, in passing, or as leaders in your community. Spend some time interceding for three of these people. Ask God to confront them with the solemn truth that there is only one way.

Lord Jesus, so often I walk among people who doubt the truth of Scripture. I confess that I too have had moments when I've questioned Your absolute authority. In a world saturated in idolatry, I pray that You will make Your way clear in my eyes and in the eyes of the people I know. Allow them to experience the narrow yet irresistible hope You so generously offer. Speak through me. Speak to me. There is ONE.

GOD'S GRACIOUS GRIP

You heard the story of Team Hoyt in the video session. This father and son make the perfect living parable. Since Rick's legs don't work, he depends entirely on the strength of his dad to push him through all those races. God wants you to do the same: "Whoever believes in him shall not perish but have eternal life" (John 3:16).

Team Hoyt

1 **Rick relies on his dad to get him across the finish line. In what ways is your faith dynamic with Jesus similar to Rick's dependence on his dad?**

_____

_____

We bring to the spiritual race what Rick Hoyt brings to the physical one. Our spiritual legs have no strength. Our morality has no muscle. Our good deeds cannot carry us across the finish line, but Christ can. "To the one who does not work, but believes in Him who justifies the ungodly, his faith is credited as righteousness" (Rom. 4:5, NASB).

Paul assures salvation to the most unlikely: not to the worker but to the truster, not to the affluent but to the bankrupt—the child who will trust with Rick Hoyt reliance. "Trusting-him-to-do-it is what gets you set right with God, by God. Sheer gift" (Rom. 4:5, MSG). We bring what Rick brings. And God does what Dick does. He takes start-to-finish-line responsibility for his children. The

GOD TAKES
START-TO-FINISH-
LINE RESPONSIBILITY
FOR HIS CHILDREN.

Amplified Bible translation of John 10:28 says: "I give them eternal life, and they shall never lose it or perish throughout the ages. [To all eternity they shall never by any means be destroyed.] And no one is able to snatch them out of My hand" (John 10:28).

We parents understand God's resolve. When our children stumble, we do not disown them. God, our Father, will not let us go. At the moment of salvation we "become children of God" (John 1:12, NASB). He alters our lineage; redefines our spiritual parenthood; and, in doing so, secures our salvation.

To accomplish the mission, the Father seals us with His Spirit. "Having believed, you were marked in him with a seal, the promised Holy Spirit" (Eph. 1:13). A soul sealed by God is safe.

2 Which of the following words could be used to describe the spiritual relationship you have with God once you believe and He gives you eternal life? Check all that apply.

▦ Short-term	▦ Permanent	▦ Durable
▦ Continual	▦ Fragile	▦ Enduring
▦ Uncertain	▦ For keeps	▦ Tentative
▦ Sure	▦ Reliable	▦ Undecided
▦ Forever	▦ Precarious	▦ Wavering

Go back and circle which word means the most to you.

CHRIST PAID TOO
HIGH A PRICE TO LEAVE
US UNGUARDED.

Christ paid too high a price to leave us unguarded: "Remember, he has identified you as his own, guaranteeing that you will be saved on the day of redemption" (Eph. 4:30, NLT). What a difference this assurance makes!

(#2 answers: continual, steadfast, sure, forever, permanent, for keeps, reliable, durable, enduring, perpetual)

3 Contemplate the truth of the following verses as you read them aloud. Underline the things that cannot separate you from the love of Christ. I've given you a start and underlined one.

"Can anything ever separate us from Christ's love? Does it mean he no longer loves us if we have trouble or calamity, or are persecuted, or hungry, or destitute, or in danger, or threatened with death? And I am convinced that nothing can ever separate us from God's love. Neither <u>death</u> nor life, neither angels nor demons, neither our fears for today nor our worries about tomorrow—not even the powers of hell can separate us from God's love. No power in the sky above or in the earth below—indeed, nothing in all creation will ever be able to separate us from the love of God that is revealed in Christ Jesus our Lord." Romans 8:35,38-39, NLT

Even in out darkest days, life's problems will never be able to separate us from the love of God.

4 **Did any part of Romans 8 take your breath away? Why?**

_____

_____

5 **What does the Romans 8 passage promise and not promise about the quality of our life circumstances?**

Promise: _____

_____

Not promise: _____

_____

6 **Why do you think we often interpret or attempt to confirm God's attention and nearness by our own circumstances?**

_____

_____

_____

ROMANS 8:39, NLT

"Nothing in all creation will ever be able to separate us from the love of God that is revealed in Christ Jesus our Lord."

ONLY CHRIST
GUARANTEES
A SAFE LANDING.

GOD'S GRIP
IS STRONGER
THAN YOUR SLIP.

My air-force pilot friend who forgot to buckle his seat belt lacked assurance for the duration of the flight. He said he didn't have a very good time. In the same way, eternal insecurity extracts joy from many people. Only Christ guarantees a safe landing.

No one but Jesus "buckles you in." You may slip—indeed, you will—but you will not fall. God's grip is stronger than your slip. Hence the invitation to believe "in him."

How do we begin to believe? We do what young Rick Hoyt did. We turn to our Father for help.

When Dick and Rick Hoyt cross finish lines, both receive finisher medals. Postrace listings include both names. The dad does the work, but the son shares in the victory. Why? Because he believes. And because he believes, both celebrate the finish.

May you and your Father do the same.

OUR CONVERSATION WITH GOD

Reflect on ways God has carried you since September 11, 2001. We've all experienced personal 9-11s of cancer, loss, crisis, and unbelief. The roads lead all of us through (not over) the valley of the shadow of death. But God remains. Even when we're barely able to put one foot in front of the other. He is there.

Lord, I sometimes forget You carry me. I have a tendency to believe I'm self-sufficient. Carry me into the future, Jesus. Carry me through the crooked roads and the dark valleys. I confess that You hold the world together. You beckon the sun to rise and the stars to shine. Nothing is impossible for You. May my crowns of self-sufficiency melt away under the light of Your powerful and loving gaze.

FOR DAY 5 *turn to "The 3:16 Life" on page 144 and follow the instructions for week 4.*

WE LIVE

Week 5

GROUP REVIEW OF WEEK 4

Follow the session plans in the leader guide on page 166.

1. Discuss your responses to this question from day 1 (p. 74): Have you ever been in a situation in which you trusted someone with your safety or your life? Why do you think this is a greater struggle for some people than for others?

2. If someone walked into the room right now and asked how you know for certain you have eternal life, how would you respond? How has your understanding of *belief* changed this week?

3. Who helped you understand that you can't save you, and what did that person do to help you? (See p. 81.) Whom are you helping to come to the same personal understanding? Choose a partner and pray together by name for the salvation of friends and for each other as you share God's good news.

4. How would you answer someone who tells you, "All roads lead to heaven"? Look back at day 3, activity 5 (p. 82).

5. Turn to page 87 and discuss your responses to activity 5.

VIEW DVD MESSAGE: "WE LIVE"

1. There are two destinations, and we get to choose. Some perish, and some live.
2. The Tragedy of _____
3. *Topos*—geographical location
4. Hell is outside the boundaries of heaven, the realm of conclusion, and the possibility of change.

5. If you spend your life telling God to be quiet and leave you alone, hell is that place where He honors your request.

6. How could a loving God send sinners to hell? He doesn't. They volunteer. Those who go to hell choose to go there.

7. The supreme surprise of hell is this: Christ went there so you won't have to.

8. The Triumph of _____

9. The reason you're going to love heaven is because you will be at your best forever. ... God impounds all imperfections at His gate. ... You will enjoy everyone else at their best.

10. Heaven is the perfect place of perfected people with our perfect God.

Scriptures referenced: John 3:16; Matthew 7:23; Jude 13; 2 Thessalonians 1:9; Matthew 8:12; Matthew 10:28; Luke 16:24; Acts 1:25; Matthew 22:13; Luke 16:26; Matthew 25:46; Luke 19:14; Ezekiel 33:11; Revelation 21:27; Revelation 22:3; 1 John 2:17; Isaiah 11:6; Revelation 21:4; Genesis 2:15; Revelation 22:3; Matthew 25:21; Romans 11:33

Message-notes blanks: (2) Hell; (8) Heaven

GROUP RESPONSE

1. Which statement about hell was most enlightening and why?

2. Why does the topic of hell create such resistance? Why must we discuss and understand it anyway?

3. If God doesn't want anyone to perish, why does hell exist, and why do people go there?

4. What is the most exciting description of heaven you heard and why?

5. How did God become more beautiful to you through this message on hell and heaven?

FOR GOD
SO LOVED
THE WORLD
THAT HE
GAVE HIS
ONE AND ONLY SON
THAT
WHOEVER
BELIEVES
IN HIM
SHALL NOT
PERISH
BUT HAVE
ETERNAL
LIFE.
JOHN 3:16

HIGHLIGHTS FOR WEEK 5

1. God has quarantined a precinct in His vast universe as the depository of the hard-hearted.

2. God has wrapped caution tape on hell's porch and posted a million and one red flags outside the entrance.

3. Thanks to Christ, this earth can be the nearest you come to hell. But apart from Christ, this earth is the nearest you'll come to heaven.

4. You will die and be buried. Since you will, don't you need someone who knows the way out?

DON'T FORGET TO WORK ON YOUR 3:16 STORY IN DAY 5.

"SHALL ... PERISH"

The hero of heaven is God. Angels don't worship mansions or glittering avenues. Neither gates nor jewels prompt the hosts to sing ... God does. His majesty stirs the pen of heaven's poets and the awe of her citizens. Inhabitants of heaven forever marvel at the sins God forgives, the promises He keeps, the plan He executes.

He, at this very moment, issues invitations by the millions. He whispers through the kindness of a grandparent, shouts through the tempest of a tsunami. Through the funeral He cautions, "Life is fragile." Through a sickness He reminds, "Days are numbered." God may speak through nature or nurture, majesty or mishap. But through all and to all He invites, "Come, enjoy Me forever."

1 **Read Revelation 22:17 in the margin and underline to whom God issues His invitation.**

2 **Heaven/Christianity was never meant to be an elite country club. How do you feel about this all-inclusive invitation?**

_____

3 **Why do you think Christianity is sometimes perceived as a members-only club when we're supposed to have such a wide-open membership policy?**

_____

_____

GOD INVITES, "COME, ENJOY ME FOREVER."

REVELATION 22:17

"The Spirit and the bride say, 'Come!' And let him who hears say, 'Come!' Whoever is thirsty, let him come; and whoever wishes, let him take the free gift of the water of life."

God invites; yet many people have no desire to come. They don't want anything to do with God. He speaks; they cover their ears. He commands; they scoff. They don't want Him telling them how to live. They mock what He says about marriage, money, sex, or the value of human life. They regard His Son as a joke and the cross as utter folly (see 1 Cor. 1:18).

"In them is fulfilled the prophecy of Isaiah: 'You will be ever hearing but never understanding; you will be ever seeing but never perceiving. For this people's heart has become calloused; they hardly hear with their ears, and they have closed their eyes. Otherwise they might see with their eyes, hear with their ears, understand with their hearts and turn, and I would heal them'" (Matt. 13:14-15).

4 According to Matthew 13:14-15, what happens when people repeatedly close their eyes and ears to God's invitation? Check all that apply.

- a. God angrily blows them off.
- b. Their hearts become so calloused they no longer hear God.
- c. They don't receive healing.
- d. God makes them blind and deaf.

MANY PEOPLE SPEND THEIR LIVES TELLING GOD TO LEAVE THEM ALONE. AND AT THE MOMENT OF THEIR FINAL BREATH, HE WILL HONOR THEIR REQUEST.

In the session we examined the most somber of realities: hell. Many people spend their lives telling God to leave them alone. And at the moment of their final breath, He will honor their request: "Get away from me, you who do evil. I never knew you" (Matt. 7:23, NCV).

5 What are common perceptions of hell you've held or encountered?

- a. It doesn't exist.
- b. It's a cartoon place, complete with a red, fork-tailed devil.
- c. It's only for really evil people.
- d. It's a myth designed to scare people into behaving.

Other: _____

A glimpse into the pit won't brighten your day, but it will enlighten your understanding of Jesus. He didn't avoid the discussion. Quite the contrary. He planted a one-word caution sign between you and hell's path: *perish*. "Whoever believes in him shall not perish but have eternal life" (John 3:16).

Destroy. Perish. Don't such words imply an end to suffering? I wish I could say they do. There is no point on which I'd more gladly be wrong than the eternal duration of hell. If God, on the last day, extinguishes the wicked, I'll celebrate my misreading of His words. Yet annihilation seems inconsistent with Scripture. God sobers His warnings with eternal language: "The smoke of their torment goes up forever and ever, and they have no rest, day or night" (Rev. 14:11, ESV). How could the euthanized soul "have no rest, day or night"?

Jesus parallels hell with Gehenna, a rubbish dump outside the walls of Jerusalem, infamous for its unending smoldering and decay. He employs *Gehenna* as a word picture of hell, the place where the "worm does not die and the fire is not quenched" (Mark 9:48, ESV). A deathless worm and quenchless fire—however symbolic these phrases may be—smack of the ongoing consumption of something. Jesus speaks of sinners being "thrown outside, into the darkness, where there will be weeping and gnashing of teeth" (Matt. 8:12). How can a nonexistent person weep or gnash teeth?

6 **Which of the following is the more consistent biblical view of what happens to people in hell? Check one.**

- a. They are annihilated, destroyed. They cease to exist.
- b. They continue to suffer torment with no rest from the horror.

Hell lasts as long as heaven. It may have a back door or a graduation day, but I haven't found it. Much perishes in hell. Hope perishes. Happiness perishes. But the body and soul of the God-deniers continue—outside heaven, hope, and God's goodness.

MATTHEW 25:46, RSV

"They will go away into eternal punishment, but the righteous into eternal life."

7 Jesus talked a lot about hell. Why do you think God wants us to understand hell as well as heaven?

_____

_____

_____

8 How might your answer above influence your life on earth and impact your relationship with God and others.

_____

_____

_____

YOUR CONVERSATION WITH GOD

Imagine a world without God: what it looks like, what it feels like. Spend a few moments asking God to begin to open the eyes and ears of those on the path that leads to destruction.

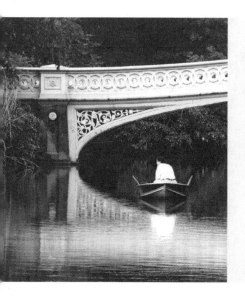

Savior Jesus, thank You for saving me from the destiny of destruction. Help me realize the brevity of life and the urgency and preeminence of the task I have been given. Teach me to see people the way You see them—lost, dying, hopeless, and blind outside Your grace. May I never forget that without You I would simply be another wreck en route to the scrap heap of eternity. Thank You for loving me, adopting me, and redeeming me. I am amazed once again by grace.

"SHALL NOT PERISH"?

Even the vilest precincts of humanity know the grace of God. People who want nothing of God still enjoy His benefits. Adolf Hitler witnessed the wonder of the Alps. Saddam Hussein enjoyed the blushing sunrise of the desert. The dictator, child molester, serial rapist, and drug peddler—all enjoy the common grace of God's goodness. They hear children laugh, smell dinner cooking, and tap their toes to the rhythm of a good song. They deny God yet enjoy His benevolence.

But these privileges are confiscated at the gateway to hell.

1 **What do you think it will mean to be "shut out from the presence" of the Lord? (See 2 Thess. 1:8-9, margin.)**

_____

_____

Hell knows none of heaven's kindnesses, no overflow of divine perks. The only laughter the unrepentant hear is evil; the only desires they know are selfish. As the Scottish professor James Denney describes it, God-rejecters "pass into a night on which no morning dawns."[1] Hell is society at its worst.

More tragically, hell is individuals at their worst. It surfaces and amplifies the ugliest traits in people. Cravings will go unchecked. Worriers will fret and never find peace. Thieves will steal and never have enough. Drunks always craving, gluttons always demanding. None will be satisfied. Remember: "their worm does not die"

> PEOPLE WHO WANT NOTHING OF GOD STILL ENJOY HIS BENEFITS.

2 THESSALONIANS 1:8-9

"He will punish those who do not know God and do not obey the gospel of our Lord Jesus. They will be punished with everlasting destruction and shut out from the presence of the Lord and from the majesty of his power."

(Mark 9:48). As one writer put it, "Not only will the unbeliever be in hell, but hell will be in him too."[2]

Death freezes the moral compass. People will remain in the fashion they enter. Revelation 22:11 seems to emphasize hell's unrepentant evil: "Let the evildoer still do evil, and the filthy still be filthy" (RSV). The Godless remain ungodly.

2 **What continuing evil practice would horrify you most about hell? Why?**

_____

_____

Hell is not a correctional facility or a reform school. Its members hear no admonishing parents, candid sermons, or Spirit of God, no voice of God, no voice of God's people. Spend a lifetime telling God to be quiet, and He'll do just that. God honors our request for silence. In Luke 19:14 the people pronounced the theme of hell: "We don't want this man to be our king." So in history's highest expression of fairness, God honors their preference.

"I willingly believe that the damned are, in one sense, successful rebels to the end; that the doors of hell are locked on the inside."
—C. S. Lewis [3]

3 **Does the C. S. Lewis quote in the margin shock or surprise you?** ▪ Yes ▪ No **How does the thought that hell's doors are "locked from the inside" change your thoughts about hell and God's justice?**

_____

_____

God, inherently holy, must exclude evil from His new universe. God, eternally gracious, never forces His will. The hearts of damned fools never soften; their minds never change: "Men were scorched with great heat, and they blasphemed the name of God who has power over these plagues; and they did not repent and give Him glory" (Rev. 16:9, NKJV).

4 **What does it mean to you that the people in Revelation 16 still refuse to repent?**

_____

_____

Contrary to the idea that hell prompts remorse, it doesn't. It intensifies blasphemy. Like the rich man in Luke 16, the people in hell want relief, but they don't want God. The rich man could see heaven but didn't request a transfer.

Even the longing for God is a gift from God, and where there is no more of God's goodness, there is no longing for Him. Though every knee shall bow before God and every tongue confess His preeminence (see Rom. 14:11), the hard-hearted will do so stubbornly and without worship. There will be no atheists in hell (see Phil. 2:10-11), but there will be no God-seekers either.

5 **Which description of hell is the most spine-chilling for you?**

- A physical place
- Eternal torment
- No rest, day or night
- Unquenched fire

- Darkness
- Society at its worst
- All evil, all the time
- No voice of goodness

Why? _____

Still we wonder, _Is the punishment fair?_ Such a penalty seems inconsistent with a God of love—overkill. Isn't God overreacting?

A man once accused me of the same. We encountered an impatient shopper at a convenience store. My three girls were selecting pastries from the doughnut shelf. They weren't moving quickly enough for him, so he leaned over their shoulders and barked, "You kids hurry up. You're taking too long." I, an aisle away, overheard the derision and approached him. "Sir, those are my

ROMANS 14:11

"It is written: ' "As surely as I live," says the Lord, "every knee will bow before me; every tongue will confess to God." ' "

Daughters and Doughnuts

3:16

16

daughters. They didn't deserve those words. You need to apologize to them."

He minimized the offense: "I didn't do anything that bad."

That verdict was not his to render. Those were my daughters he had hurt. Who was he to challenge my reaction?

Who are we to challenge God's? Only He knows the full story, the number of invitations the stubborn-hearted have refused and the slander they've spewed.

6 According to 2 Peter 3:9, can anyone legitimately charge God with being unfair? Explain.

_____

_____

_____

God has wrapped caution tape on hell's porch and posted a million and one red flags outside the entrance. To descend its stairs, you'd have to cover your ears; blindfold your eyes; and, most of all, ignore the epic sacrifice of history: Christ, in God's hell on humanity's cross, crying out to the blackened sky, "My God, my God, why have you forsaken me?" (Matt. 27:46).

The supreme surprise of hell is this: Christ went there on the cross so that you won't have to. Yet hell could not contain Him. He arose not just from the dead but from the depths: "Through death He [destroyed] him who had the power of death, that is, the devil" (Heb. 2:14, NKJV).

7 Read the passages from Revelation in the margin. What did Christ bring with Him when He emerged from Satan's domain? Why did this matter?

_____

_____

_____

2 PETER 3:9

"He is patient with you, not wanting anyone to perish, but everyone to come to repentance."

■

REVELATION 1:18, NKJV

"I have the keys of Hades and of Death."

■

REVELATION 3:7

"These are the words of him who is holy and true, who holds the key of David. What he opens no one can shut, and what he shuts no one can open."

Christ is the warden of eternity. The door He shuts, no one opens. The door He opens, no one shuts (see Rev. 3:7). We face death with either fear or faith, dread or joy. "Whoever believes in him shall not perish." God makes the offer. We make the choice.

8 **How do you think the child of God faces the moment of death differently than the person who doesn't know Christ? Explain your answer.**

_____

_____

_____

_____

YOUR CONVERSATION WITH GOD

Ask God to help you identify those times when you are living outside the faith and joy He offers and embracing the fear and dread that Jesus remedied on the cross. Ask Father God to help you to be an ambassador of joy as you encounter people living in fear and dread.

2 THESSALONIANS
4:13, HCSB

"We do not want you to be uninformed, brothers, concerning those who are asleep, so that you will not grieve like the rest, who have no hope."

Father, banish me from returning to fear and dread. It's so easy for me to worry, to obsess, to yearn pointlessly for false security. You have called me to live in faith and in joy. I pray that my life will be an example of triumph through tears, hope in darkness, and faith in a land of squalor. It seems that many times I live on the edge of hell—empty of joy, light, holy affection. Teach me to crash the gates of hell with the hope and overcome darkness until the dawn appears! Indeed, You are my bright and morning star. Shine, dear Father, so that I can see the way. Jesus, I rest in Your escape.

In one of his "Far Side" cartoons, Gary Larson depicts a winged man seated in heaven on a cloud. No one near. Nothing to do. Marooned on his celestial post. The caption witnesses his despair: "Wish I'd brought a magazine."[4]

We can relate. Eternal life? Clouds in our midst, harps on our laps, and time on our hands, unending time. Forever and ever. Nonstop. An endless sing-along. A hymn, then a chorus, then still more verses. Hmm ... that's it? "Whatever the tortures of hell," declared Isaac Asimov, "I think the boredom of heaven would be even worse."[5]

1 **As you have thought about heaven in the past, what are some of the thoughts that honestly make it somewhat unappealing?**

_____

_____

WILL ETERNITY
MEET EXPECTATIONS?

Will eternity meet expectations? Can heaven deliver on its promises? Jesus gives an assuring response to such questions:

"Don't let your hearts be troubled. Trust in God, and trust also in me. There is more than enough room in my Father's home. If this were not so, would I have told you that I am going to prepare a place for you? When everything is ready, I will come and get you, so that you will always be with me where I am" (John 14:1-3, NLT).

2 **How do you envision heaven? Mansions? Streets of gold? Describe your thoughts.**

_____

_____

The movies have told you wrong. Those images of knee-high fog banks, disembodied friends, and floating spirits? Forget them. Like hell, heaven is tangible and touchable: as real as the soil in your garden, as physical as the fruit in your orchard. In fact, your garden and fruit might look familiar in heaven.

CREATION'S DELIVERY DAY

We assume God will destroy this universe and relocate His children ... but why would He? Why obliterate a work of art? God never denounced His earth, just our mistreatment of it. Besides, God is the God of reclamation, not extermination. He restores, recovers, renews. Expect and look for Him to do it again—to renew and reclaim every square inch of what is rightfully His.

But what about the promises of the earth's destruction? Peter and John use A-bomb terminology: "Disappear with a roar ... destroyed by fire ... laid bare ... passed away" (2 Pet. 3:10; Rev. 21:1). Won't this planet be destroyed? Yes, but destruction need not mean elimination. Our bodies provide a prototype. They will pass away, return to dust. Yet Christ will reverse decomposition with resurrection. Amino acids will regenerate. Lungs will awaken. Molecules will reconnect.

3 **Read 1 Corinthians 15:52-53 in the margin and underline what will happen to the living and the dead when the last trumpet sounds.**

1 CORINTHIANS 15:52-53

"... in a flash, in the twinkling of an eye, at the last trumpet. For the trumpet will sound, the dead will be raised imperishable, and we will be changed. For the perishable must clothe itself with the imperishable, and the mortal with immortality."

The mortal body will put on immortality. We'll be raised and changed. We'll move from perishable to imperishable. The same is true about earth: "The creation itself will be liberated from its bondage to decay and brought into the glorious freedom of the children of God" (Rom. 8:21).

AN ETERNAL, PERFECT YOU!

You will be you at your best forever. Even now you have your good moments. Occasional glimpses of your heavenly self. When you change your baby's diaper, forgive your boss's temper, tolerate your spouse's moodiness, you display traces of saintliness. It's the other moments that sour life. Tongue as sharp as a razor. Moods as unpredictable as Mount Saint Helens. This part wearies you.

But God impounds imperfections at His gate. His light silences the wolfman within: "Nothing unworthy will be allowed to enter [the city]" (v. 27, CEV). Pause and let this promise drench you. Can you envision your sinless existence? For a wonderful exploration of the new heavens and the new earth, let me recommend Randy Alcorn's study called *Heaven*.[6]

GOD IMPOUNDS IMPERFECTIONS AT HIS GATE.

4 **What are some of the imperfect things about you that you will be most glad to be rid of in heaven? Why?**

_____

_____

Just think what Satan has taken from you, even in the last few hours. You worried about a decision and envied someone's success, dreaded a conversation and resented an interruption. He's been prowling your environs all day, pickpocketing peace, joy, belly laughs, and honest love. Rotten freebooter.

But his days are numbered. Unlike in the garden of Eden, Satan will not lurk in heaven's gardens: "There shall be no more curse" (22:3, NKJV). He will not tempt; hence, you will not stumble: "The world is passing away, and the lust of it; but he who does the will of God abides forever" (1 John 2:17, NKJV).

You will be you at your best forever! "Dear friends, now we are children of God, and what we will be has not yet been made known. But we know that when he appears, we shall be like him, for we shall see him as he is" (1 John 3:2).

YOU WILL BE YOU AT YOUR BEST FOREVER.

5 **We'll be like Christ. To which Christlike character traits, expressed uniquely through you, do you most eagerly look forward?**

▪ Pure	▪ Gentle	▪ Humble	▪ Peaceable
▪ Entreatable	▪ Merciful	▪ Loving	▪ Honest
▪ Steadfast	▪ Patient	▪ Giving	▪ Faithful
▪ Obedient	▪ Meek	▪ Sinless	▪ Holy
▪ Joyful	▪ Wise	▪ Just	▪ Forgiving

Other: _____

Not only will you be at your best, but you'll enjoy everyone else at their best! As it is, one of us is always a step behind. Bad moods infect the best of families. Complaints shadow the clearest days. Bad apples spoil bunches of us, but rotten fruit doesn't qualify for the produce section of heaven.

YOU'LL ENJOY EVERYONE ELSE AT THEIR BEST!

Christ will have completed His redemptive work. All gossip excised and jealousy extracted. You'll love the result. No one will doubt your word, question your motives, or speak evil behind your back. God's sin purging discontinues all strife.

6 **What hurtful or destructive attitude or action of others will you be most glad never to experience again? Why?**

_____

_____

_____

No sin means no thieves, no divorce, no heartbreak, and no boredom. You won't be bored in heaven, because you won't be the same you in heaven. Boredom emerges from soils that heaven disallows. The soil of weariness: our eyes tire. Mental limitations: information overload dulls us. Self-centeredness: we grow disinterested when the spotlight shifts to others. Tedium: meaningless activity siphons vigor.

Satan will take these weedy soils to hell with him, leaving you with a keen mind, endless focus, and God-honoring assignments.

Yes, you will have assignments in heaven. What do His happy children do but serve Him? We might serve in the capacity we serve now. Couldn't earthly assignments hint at heavenly ones?

One thing is sure: you'll love it. Never weary, selfish, or defeated. Clear mind, tireless muscles, unhindered joy.

AN INFINITE GOD

Don't assume we will exhaust our study of God in heaven. Endless attributes await us. His grace will increasingly stun, wisdom progressively astound, and perfection ever more sharpen into focus.

We serve a God so rapt with wonders that their viewing requires an eternity. A God whose beauty enhances with proximity:

"Many, O LORD my God,
  are the wonders you have done.
The things you planned for us
  no one can recount to you;
were I to speak and tell of them,
  they would be too many to declare" (Ps. 40:5).

HIS GRACE WILL INCREASINGLY STUN, WISDOM PROGRESSIVELY ASTOUND, AND PERFECTION EVER MORE SHARPEN INTO FOCUS.

7 Why do you think we'll need all of eternity to really know and understand God?

_____
_____
_____

AN ETERNAL HOME

John Todd was very young when the deaths of his parents left him orphaned. He was one of several children, and, as was common in the early 1800s, he and all his siblings were farmed out to relatives. An aunt offered to take little John. She sent a servant by the name of Caesar to bring John to her. The boy climbed on the back of the horse, wrapped his small arms around the man, and set out for her house. His questions unveiled his fears.

"Will she be there?"

"Oh, yes," Caesar assured. "She'll be there waiting up for you."

"Will I like living with her?"

"My son, you fall into good hands."

"Will she love me?"

The servant was patient and soft in his reply: "Ah, she has a big heart."

"Do you think she'll go to bed before we get there?"

"Oh, no! She'll be sure to wait up for you. You'll see when we get out of these woods. You'll see her candle in the window."

Sure enough, as they neared the house, John saw a candle in the window and his aunt standing in the doorway. As he shyly approached the porch, she reached down and kissed him and said, "Welcome home!"

Young John Todd grew up in his aunt's care. She was a mother to him. When the time came for him to select a profession, he followed a calling into the pastorate. Years later, the role with his aunt was reversed. She sent news of her failing health and impending death. Here is what he wrote in reply:

My Dear Aunt,

Years ago, I left a house of death, not knowing where I was to go, whether anyone cared, whether it was the end of me. The ride was long, but the servant encouraged me. Finally I arrived to your embrace and a new home. I was expected; I felt safe. You did it all for me.

Now it's your turn to go. I'm writing to let you know, someone is waiting up, your room is all ready, the light is on, the door is open, and you're expected![7]

YOUR CONVERSATION WITH GOD

Ask God to foreshadow your life with the extreme makeover you'll experience in heaven! Take time before God to imagine a new Earth unaffected by the ugliness evil creates. Focus on how you can bring a slice of the Kingdom on Earth as it is in heaven.

Lord, I'm so ready to see the superstructure of Satan's domain implode as You silence him and his unholy cronies at the end of this age. But Lord, I'm not satisfied with just waiting for the sweet by and by. I want Your kingdom to reign here on earth in my life and in this world. Flood my life with refreshing streams of purity, faithfulness, joy, and all the riches of a believer's life surrendered to You. Lord, today when I hear complaints, when I am disturbed by the ugliness of this world, when I am reminded of starvation, war, divorce, disease, shame, rejection, poverty, and perversion, remind me that this is just a breath in the scope of eternity. Help me make my life count. May Your truth march on!

"LIFE"

day four

Life has letdowns. How do you know Christ won't be one of them? Honestly. Dare you believe that He gives what He promises? Life. Eternal life. "Whoever believes in him shall not perish but have eternal life" (John 3:16). We're pulling into the final station.

1   **See if you can fill in the blanks to our outline of this most famous verse in the Bible.**

God _____.

God _____.

We _____.

We _____.

Loves, gave, believe. Having worked our way through the 3:16 itinerary, we need to ponder one more word: *life.* When we believe we live, we have eternal life.

Beer companies offer you life in their hops. Perfume makers promise new life for your romance. But don't confuse costume jewelry with God's sapphire.

Jesus offers *zoe,* the Greek word for "life as God has it."[8] Whereas *bios,* its sibling term, is life extensive, *zoe* is life intensive. Jesus talks less about life's duration and more about its quality, vitality, energy, and fulfillment:

> **"I have come that they may have life, and have it to the full" (John 10:10).**

ZOE

Greek word meaning "life as God has it, life intensive"

BIOS

Greek word meaning "duration of life, life extensive"

109

2 Since the word for *life* in John 3:16 is *zoe*, what do you think are the implications?

_____

_____

3 Given that Jesus guaranteed hardship, what do you think He meant by abundant life?

_____

_____

What the new mate, sports car, or unexpected check could never do, Christ says, "I can." You'll love how He achieves it. He reconnects your soul with God.

A LIVING SOUL

What God gave Adam and Eve, He entrusted to you and me. A soul. "The LORD God formed man of the dust of the ground, and breathed into his nostrils the breath of life; and man became a living being" (Gen. 2:7, NKJV).

You, a bipedal ape? Chemical fluke? Atomic surprise? By no means. You bear the very breath of God. He exhaled Himself into you, making you a "living being" (v. 7).

The Hebrew word translated here in Genesis 2 as *being* is *nephesh,* which appears more than 750 times in the Bible. It sometimes refers to the life force present in all creatures. In the context of a person, however, *nephesh* refers to our souls.[9]

Your soul distinguishes you from zoo dwellers. God gave the camel a hump and the giraffe a flagpole neck, but He reserved His breath, or a soul, for you.

NEPHESH

Hebrew word meaning
a living soul

4 Read Genesis 1:27 (right page margin) and complete the statement: Because God breathed life into me, I am ...

_____

How does that make you feel about the person God created you to be? You bear His stamp. You are the image of God. You do things God does. Think. Question. Reflect. You blueprint buildings, chart sea crossings, and swallow throat lumps when your kids say their alphabet. You, like Adam, have a soul.

A DISCONNECTED SOUL

And, like Adam, you've used your soul to disobey God. God's command to the charter couple includes the Bible's first reference to death: "You must not eat from the tree of the knowledge of good and evil, for when you eat of it you will surely die" (Gen. 2:17).

My daughter Andrea, when elementary-school age, asked a grown-up question: "Dad, if God didn't want them to eat from the tree, why did He put it there?" The answer, best I can tell, is to remind us who created whom. When we attempt to swap roles with God and tell Him we can eat (think, say, do, own, hurt, inhale, ingest, demand) anything we want, we die two deaths. Adam and Eve died physically, eventually. Spiritually they died instantly.

Their bodies continued to function, but their hearts hardened. They stopped trusting God. Their friendship with their Maker died. We understand how this happened. If you loan me your car and I wreck it, will I want to see you again? No. I will dread our next encounter. Adam and Eve experienced the same.

Prior to disobeying God, He spoke; they listened. He gave assignments; they fulfilled them. They were naked but unashamed, transparent and unafraid. Yet as one drop of ink clouds a glass of water, the stubborn deed darkened their souls. Everything changed. God's presence stirred panic, not peace. Adam ran like a kid caught raiding the pantry. "I was afraid" (Gen. 3:10). Intimacy with God ceased; separation from God began.

We'll always wonder why Adam didn't ask for forgiveness. But he didn't, and the guilty pair was "banished ... from the Garden of Eden" (Gen. 3:23). We've loitered outside the gates ever since.

GENESIS 1:27

"God created man in his own image, in the image of God he created him; male and female he created them."

WHEN WE ATTEMPT TO SWAP ROLES WITH GOD AND TELL HIM WE CAN DO ANYTHING WE WANT, WE DIE TWO DEATHS.

5 Think of some times or ways you have responded to God or an authority in similar ways to Adam and Eve. Write a brief note below each action below.

1. I felt guilt or shame and tried a cover-up…

_____

2. I blamed someone else…

_____

3. Because of fear, guilt, and shame, I avoided God…

_____

Deep within we've known (haven't we known?) something is awry—we feel disconnected. What we hope will bring life leaves us longing for something more. Our dissatisfaction mates with disappointment and gives birth to some unruly children: drunkenness, power plays, 80-hour workweeks, nosedives into sexual perversions—all nothing more than poorly disguised longings for Eden. We long to restore what Adam lost.

A RECONNECTED LIFE

JESUS STEPS FORTH WITH A RECONNECTION INVITATION.

Jesus steps forth with a reconnection invitation: "Because of his great love for us, God, who is rich in mercy, made us alive with Christ even when we were dead in transgressions—it is by grace you have been saved" (Eph. 2:4-5).

6 List areas of your life or choices you have made that resulted in becoming disconnected from God?

_____

_____

7 What do you think it takes to get reconnected? What's the difference between connecting and reconnecting?

_____

_____

Though we are dead in our transgressions and sins and separated from the life of God, whoever believes that Jesus is the Christ is born of God. Reborn! This is not a physical birth resulting from human passion or plan—this rebirth comes from God (see Eph. 2:1; 4:18; 1 John 5:1, NKJV; John 1:13, NLT).

Don't miss the invisible, inward miracle triggered by belief. God reinstates us to garden-of-Eden status. What Adam and Eve did, we now do! The flagship family walked with God; we can too. They heard His voice; so can we. They were naked and unashamed; we can be transparent and unafraid. No more running or hiding.

Can Jesus actually replace death with life? He did a convincing job with His own. We can trust Him because He has been there.

On a trip to China, I rode past Tiananmen Square in a bus full of Westerners. We tried to recollect the causes and consequences of the revolt. Our knowledge of history was embarrassing. One gave one date; another gave a different one. One person remembered a certain death toll; someone else disagreed. All this time our translator remained silent.

Finally one of us asked her, "Do you remember anything about the Tiananmen Square revolt?"

Her answer was solemn: "Yes, I was a part of it." We quickly grew quiet as she gave firsthand recollections of the bloodshed and oppression. We listened because she'd been there.

We who follow Christ do so for the same reason. He's been there … He's been to Bethlehem, wearing barn rags and hearing sheep crunch. Suckling milk and shivering against the cold. All of divinity cocooned in an eight-pound body sleeping on a cow's supper. Millions who face the chill of empty pockets or the fears of sudden change turn to Christ. Why?

Because He's been there.

He's been to Nazareth, where He made deadlines and paid bills; to Galilee, where He recruited direct reports and separated

WE LISTENED BECAUSE
SHE'D BEEN THERE.

fighters; to Jerusalem, where He stared down critics and stood up against cynics.

Why seek Jesus' help with your challenges? Because He's been there. To Nazareth, to Galilee, to Jerusalem.

But most of all, He's been to the grave. Not as a visitor but as a corpse. Buried amid the cadavers. Numbered among the dead. Heart silent and lungs vacant. Body wrapped and grave sealed. The cemetery. He's been buried there.

You haven't yet. But you will be. And since you will, don't you need someone who knows the way out?

YOUR CONVERSATION WITH GOD

Worship Jesus today by remembering that He didn't blare down instructions to us about all our sins. He didn't shame, or smirk. He came down to dusty, war-torn, heartbroken humanity and taught us how to live. Even beyond that, remember how He came to die so we could be made right.

O Jesus! You came down to eat, laugh, weep, teach, bleed, and die for people. You came to walk with us so that we could eternally walk with You. A Baby born—outcast and obscure— You were still Jesus. Master Craftsman of the universe born a carpenter's Son—You were still Jesus. Walked in the wilderness for 40 days hungry and alone—You were still Jesus. In a borrowed tomb, casualty of my sin—You were still Jesus. In the middle of my struggles, in the center of my life, in my dreams, tears, brokenness, and fears—You are still Jesus. Comforting, guiding, loving, filling, and forgiving—You are still Jesus. Holy. Beautiful. Amazing. Thank You, resurrected Savior!

FOR DAY 5 *turn to "The 3:16 Life" on page 148 and follow the instructions for week 5.*

GOD'S WHOEVER POLICY

Week 6

GROUP REVIEW OF WEEK 5

Follow the session plans in the leader guide on page 168.

1. What common perceptions of hell did you identify (day 1, activity 5, p. 94)? Why do you think some people prefer to delude themselves with these sanitized versions rather than believe in the real hell? What have you learned about heaven or hell this week that has been most life-changing?

2. How do you sense God leading you to guide others to face death—as well as the everyday struggles of life—with faith and joy? Share your thoughts from day 2, activity 8 (p. 101). What does it mean to you that Satan's "days are numbered" (see p. 104)?

3. What are some common reservations about heaven? How did Jesus address these concerns (pp. 102–3)? What do you most anticipate about heaven?

4. How does the phrase "because He's been there" give you life and hope (day 4, p. 113)?

5. Share your 3:16 story (day 5). Pray that God would give you opportunities to share your story with an unbeliever this week. Commit to support each other in prayer as you seek to share the hope of 3:16 with a hurting world.

VIEW DVD MESSAGE:
"GOD'S WHOEVER POLICY"

1. God loves. God gave. We believe. We live.
2. The word *whoever* throws open the gates of heaven to anyone who has ever lived.

3. God exports His grace worldwide.

4. *Whoever* means _____.

5. You don't have to clean up. You don't have to climb up. All you have to do is look up.

6. *Whoever* means _____.

7. God's offer has not expired. It's not too late.

8. Deathbed converts and lifelong saints enter heaven by the same gate.

9. *Whoever* means _____.

10. You've never wandered too far from God to come home.

11. You have never lost your place on God's whoever list.

12. No status is too low. No hour is too late. No place is too far. ... *Whoever* means you with Him forever!

Scriptures referenced: John 3:16; Matthew 10:32; Matthew 10:39;
Mark 3:35; Mark 16:16; John 3:36; John 4:14; John 6:37; John 11:26;
Revelation 22:17; Titus 2:11; 1 Timothy 2:6; 2 Peter 3:9; Luke 16:19-23;
Matthew 20:2; Matthew 20:10; Matthew 20:15; Luke 15:13; Luke 15:18

Message-notes blanks: (4) however; (6) whenever; (9) wherever

GROUP RESPONSE

1. What statement, Scripture, or illustration was most meaningful to you and why?

2. What barriers does the word *whoever* in John 3:16 break down? Discuss ways some try to restrict the "whoever" intent of this verse.

3. What is the message of the parable of the laborers? How does this message defy conventional wisdom?

4. Explain the however, whenever, and wherever of the prodigal son's story.

5. Have you responded to God's whoever policy by believing in Christ? If so, when and how? If not, will you do so now?

FOR GOD
SO LOVED
THE WORLD
THAT HE
GAVE HIS

ONE AND ONLY SON

THAT

WHOEVER

BELIEVES
IN HIM
SHALL NOT
PERISH
BUT HAVE
ETERNAL

LIFE.

JOHN 3:16

HIGHLIGHTS FOR WEEK 6

1. *Whoever* unrolls the welcome mat of heaven to humanity.

2. God takes you however He finds you. No need to clean up or climb up. Just look up.

3. Whenever you hear God's voice, He welcomes your response.

4. Deathbed converts and lifelong saints enter heaven by the same gate.

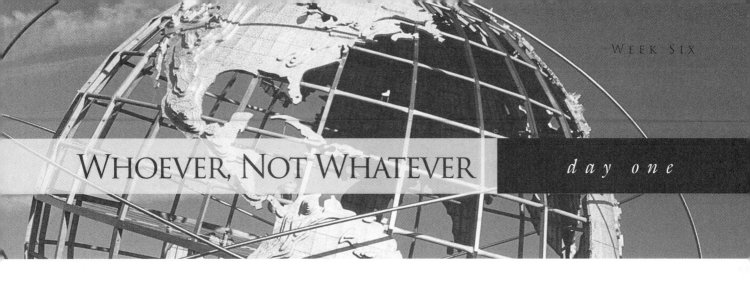

WHOEVER, NOT WHATEVER

day one

When I read F. W. Boreham's account of Cleopatra's Needle, I thought, *What a fitting way to begin our final week on God's greatest Scripture*. On September 12, 1878, the British government planted that monument from ancient Egypt in English soil and assigned it vigil over the Thames River.

At the monument's base they placed a time capsule containing one verse from the Bible in 215 languages: "For God so loved the world that he gave his one and only son, that whoever believes in him shall not perish but have eternal life."[1]

I couldn't help but picture a rummager of some future London digging through rocks and rubble finding and reading the verse. Except for one word, she might dismiss it as an old myth. *Whoever.*

Whoever unfurls 3:16 as a banner for the ages. *Whoever* unrolls the welcome mat of heaven to humanity. *Whoever* invites the world to God. As I've said, of all the words of this great verse, for me *whoever* is the best.

WHOEVER UNROLLS THE WELCOME MAT OF HEAVEN TO HUMANITY.

1 **How about you? Which of the words do you love most?**

_____

Do you have a story or reason for that choice?

_____

_____

_____

2 Have you ever been rejected, turned away, or experienced discrimination because you didn't measure up to some expressed or unstated criteria? Check any of the following areas in which you didn't qualify.

- Age (too young or too old)
- Race (wrong color or ethnic origin)
- Education (not enough or overqualified)
- Language, nationality, or citizenship
- Social status (wrong side of the tracks, wrong caste)
- Wealth/finances (below the minimum or over the maximum)
- Gender or marital status

How did you feel when you were rejected?

_____

_____

Jesus could have so easily narrowed the scope for His invitation, changing *whoever* into *whatever*. "Whatever Jew believes" or "Whatever woman follows me." But He used no qualifier. The pronoun is wonderfully indefinite. After all, who isn't a whoever?

The word sledgehammers racial fences and dynamites social classes. It bypasses gender borders and surpasses ancient traditions. *Whoever* makes it clear: God exports His grace worldwide.

AFTER ALL, WHO
ISN'T A WHOEVER?

3 As you read the following verses, circle the word *whoever* each time it occurs. Underline the phrases that tell what happens to "whoever" when they act in the way described. I've underlined one for you.

1. *"Whoever acknowledges me before men, I will also acknowledge him before my Father in heaven."* Matthew 10:32
2. *"Whoever finds his life will lose it, and whoever loses his life for my sake will find it."* Matthew 10:39

3. *"Whoever does God's will is my brother and sister and mother."* Mark 3:35

4. *"Whoever believes and is baptized will be saved, but whoever does not believe will be condemned."* Mark 16:16

5. *"Whoever believes in the Son has eternal life, but whoever rejects the Son will not see life, for God's wrath remains on him."* John 3:36

6. *"Whoever drinks the water I give him will never thirst."* John 4:14

7. *"Whoever comes to me I will never drive away."* John 6:37

8. *"Whoever lives and believes in me will never die."* John 11:26

9. *"Whoever is thirsty, let him come; and whoever wishes, let him take the free gift of the water of life."* Revelation 22:17

4 **Choose the verse that is most meaningful to you and explain why in the margin beside the verse.**

YOUR CONVERSATION WITH GOD

Reflect on the grandest invitation ever known: "Whoever." If you are weary—come. If you are tired of the hurried pace—come. He is offering us the greatest gift we could receive. No exclusion, no take-backs, no hidden catches. He just says COME!

Father God, thank You for not giving up on the world. You haven't closed the passageway to Your kingdom. Lord, I confess that sometimes I take it for granted. I am around people every day who are included in the "whoever," and I don't say a word to draw them closer to You. Forgive me for my hidden partiality and subtle prejudices. Teach me to see everyone the way You see them. Give me a passion to spread the message to whoever. They aren't hard to find. Make me a passionate messenger of your relentless, scandalous love for the world.

HOWEVER & WHENEVER

1 **Turn in your Bible and read the story of the rich man and Lazarus in Luke 16:19-31.**

Whoever Means However

The downturns of life can leave us wondering whether God still wants us. Surely Lazarus the beggar wondered. Jesus tells us he was "covered with sores and longing to eat what fell from the rich man's table. Even the dogs came and licked his sores" (Luke 16:19-21).

The two men indwell opposite sides of the city tracks. The rich man lives in posh luxury and wears the finest clothing. The language suggests he uses fabric worth its weight in gold.[2] He eats exotic food, enjoys a spacious house with botanical gardens. He's the New Testament version of a Monaco billionaire.

Lazarus is a homeless street sleeper. Dogs lick his sores. He languishes outside the mansion, hoping for scraps. Infected. Rejected. No possessions. No family.

2 **If your community took a vote on which of these two men ought to get into heaven, who do you think would get the most votes? In the margin explain your choice.**

▪ a. Rich man ▪ b. Lazarus

Wouldn't most people pick the rich and successful man who seemed to have his act together? People tend to measure acceptability by looking on outward appearance. Lazarus is an exception to God's whoever policy, right? Wrong.

In sudden drama the curtain of death falls on act 1, and eternal destiny is revealed in act 2: "The time came when the beggar died and the angels carried him to Abraham's side. The rich man also died and was buried. In hell, where he was in torment, he looked up and saw Abraham far away, with Lazarus by his side" (vv. 22-23).

Just-poor Lazarus now needs nothing. The now-poor rich man needs everything. He loses the lap of luxury, and Lazarus discovers the lap of Abraham.

Lazaruses still populate our planet. You may be one. Not begging for bread but struggling to buy some. Not sleeping on streets but on the floor perhaps? In your car sometimes? On someone else's couch often? Does God have a place for people in your place?

3 **Have you ever had any reasons for questioning whether God's whoever policy applies to you? Check all that apply.**

▓ a. I've been too bad, sinned too much.

▓ b. I'm too poor. I have nothing to offer Him.

▓ c. I'm too old. What would He want me for?

▓ d. I'm too dumb. I don't understand, can't speak clearly, …

▓ e. I'm too feeble, disabled, bedridden …

▓ f. I'm unskilled. What could I do for Him?

▓ g. I'm the wrong race. Wouldn't He prefer someone who is …

Others? Why? _____

_____

_____

_____

_____

Of all the messages this account conveys, don't miss this one: God takes you however He finds you. No need to clean up or climb up. Just look up. God's whoever policy has a however benefit.

GOD TAKES YOU HOWEVER HE FINDS YOU.

4 **How do you feel about God's whoever policy for you?**

_____

_____

Whoever Means Whenever

Not only does God's whoever policy have a however benefit, but it also features a whenever clause. Whenever you hear God's voice, He welcomes your response.

Remember the story from our session of the expired gift certificate? I had waited too long. But you haven't. Jesus considered our knowing so important that He told one of His most scandalous parables to convince us. Some have called it His parable of 11th-hour grace—the parable of the laborers in the vineyard from Matthew 20:1-16.

If you consider the story, you can't help but be just a little bothered by it. Something in us resists such grace. We identify a bit with the workers who endured the heat of the day.

5 **If you were the landowner, how much would you pay the workers if the first ones agreed to one dollar a day?**

_____ Workers starting at 6:00 a.m. (12 hours worked)

_____ Workers starting at 9:00 a.m. (9 hours worked)

_____ Workers starting at noon (6 hours worked)

_____ Workers starting at 3:00 p.m. (3 hours worked)

_____ Workers starting at 5:00 p.m. (1 hour worked)

Read Jesus's punch line to the story: "They got the same, each of them one dollar" (v. 10, MSG).

No landlord issues a final-hour invitation, does he? God does. No one pays a day's wage to one-hour workers, does he? God does. Here's the whenever clause to God's whoever policy: deathbed converts and lifelong saints enter heaven by the same gate.

DEATHBED CONVERTS
AND LIFELONG SAINTS
ENTER HEAVEN
BY THE SAME GATE.

6 Have you struggled with either of these distortions?

- If you don't come to Christ when you first sense His invitation, you may miss your opportunity. Then it will be too late to accept His offer of eternal life.
- People who do not accept Christ until very late in life won't get to heaven because they didn't have time to serve Jesus.

What other distortions of God's all-inclusive invitation would you add to the list?

_____

_____

_____

YOUR CONVERSATION WITH GOD

What have you done that seemed unforgivable? It isn't! God's grace is far greater that your sin. To think otherwise questions His sovereignty. Imagine God speaking to you: "I paid the price for you, so stop being consumed with fear. I know everything about you—every cell, every weakness, every moment of your past, present, and future. When you gasp in the whitewater rapids of tough times, I'm there. The rivers will not swallow you. And the fire? I'm ahead of you on that one. Flames may come but you are completely covered by My fireproof grace. I will be there!"

Lord, teach me to revel in the victory of Your grace. Tune my heart to sing it! Jesus, I've been so programmed in this culture to clock-punching, penny saved, penny earned living. I am fearfully in awe of the kind of grace that says no matter who you are, no matter what you've done ... I AM enough! Be my Lord. Jesus, be my Savior! Amen.

WHENEVER & WHEREVER

In the session you heard about my Uncle Billy and our talk about Jesus while my uncle was on his deathbed. Our brief talk ended with a prayer for grace. We both said, "Amen," and I soon left. Uncle Billy died within days.

1 **Do you have an "Uncle Billy" story of your own, maybe somebody you prayed over for years before seeing them finally come to Christ? If so, would you tell your story?**

_____

_____

_____

2 **Are you still praying for an "Uncle Billy"? What does Jesus' parable of 11ᵗʰ-hour grace tell you?**

_____

Did my Uncle Billy wake up in heaven? According to the parable of the 11ᵗʰ-hour workers, he did.

Some struggle with such a thought. A last-minute confessor receives the same grace as a lifetime servant? Doesn't seem fair. The workers in the parable complained too. So the landowner, and God, explained the prerogative of ownership: "Am I not allowed to do what I choose with what belongs to me?" (Matt. 20:15, RSV).

Request grace with your dying breath, and God hears your prayer. *Whoever* means *whenever.*

REQUEST GRACE WITH YOUR DYING BREATH, AND GOD HEARS YOUR PRAYER.

3 When does God hear the prayer of a sinner who comes believing in Jesus and wanting to be saved? Check all that apply.

- When they're young
- When they're old
- When they're sick
- When they're well
- When they have years to serve Him
- When they will not live to see tomorrow's sunrise

4 If you are still struggling with this whenever clause, write your questions or concerns in the margin.

WHOEVER MEANS WHEREVER

However. Whenever. And one more: *whoever* means *wherever*. Wherever you are, you're not too far to come home.

The prodigal son assumed he was. He had spurned his father's kindness and "journeyed to a far country, and there wasted his possessions with prodigal living" (Luke 15:13, NKJV).

The word translated here as *wasted* is *diaskorpizo,* the same Greek verb used to describe the action of a seed-sowing farmer. Envision him throwing handfuls of seeds onto tilled earth. Envision the prodigal tossing his father's money to greedy merchants: a roll of bills at one club, a handful of coins at another. He rides the magic carpet of cash from one party to the next. And then one day his wallet grows thin.

The credit card comes back. The maître d' says, "No"; the hotel says, "Go"; and the boy says, "Uh-oh." He slides from high hog at the trough to low pig in the mud. He finds employment feeding swine. Not a recommended career path for a Jewish boy.

5 What are some ways we get so far from God that we think we've gone too far to ever come home?

_____

_____

WASTED

To scatter abroad, disperse, to winnow—to throw the grain a considerable distance or up into the air[3]

The hunger so gnaws at the prodigal son's gut that he considers eating with the pigs. But rather than swallow the pods, he swallows his pride and begins that famous walk homeward, rehearsing a repentance speech with each step. Turns out he didn't need it: "His father saw him and had compassion, and ran and fell on his neck and kissed him" (v. 20, NKJV). The father was saving the son's place.

> IF HEAVEN'S BANQUET TABLE HAS NAMEPLATES, ONE BEARS YOUR NAME.

He's saving yours too. If heaven's banquet table has nameplates, one bears your name.

We lose much in life—sobriety, solvency, and sanity. We lose jobs and chances, and we lose at love. We lose youth and its vigor, idealism and its dreams. We lose much, but we never lose our place on God's whoever list.

YOUR CONVERSATION WITH GOD

Reflect on times when your prodigal nature revealed itself. Have you ever found yourself in a pigpen of your own making? Very few of us remain on the homestead throughout our lives. When have you lived in the far country? Perhaps you are there now. Perhaps you've been running from God. Stop dodging the love of God. Spend time right now in conversation with the Father who scans the horizon for His beloved prodigals. If you are one of them, He really is waiting and watching.

I'm so blessed to have a Father who doesn't lock the door and turn off the porch light when I am away from Him. Thank You for watching and waiting. Any exile from You is of my own making. And so, Father, I run to You. Thanks for accepting me even when the soil and the stench of my life are so embarrassing and obvious. I don't understand that kind of love, but I want to say thank You for allowing me to experience it.

GOD'S INVITATION

day four

Did you smile, at least a little bit, over Denalyn's strawberry cake? Every one of us probably has a favorite treat and has had to wait to hear whether we must pass on the pleasure or go ahead and dig in.

What a joy when we hear *whoever*. I so hope you have heard and responded. *Whoever* is God's wonderful word of welcome.

WHOEVER IS GOD'S WONDERFUL WORD OF WELCOME.

1 **Match the characteristics of God's whoever policy on the left with the corresponding application on the right. Write a letter beside each number.**

___ 1. However   a. No hour is too late.

___ 2. Whenever   b. No place is too far.

___ 3. Wherever   c. No status is too low.

However. Whenever. Wherever. *Whoever* includes you ... forever.

"Free flight: Rio de Janeiro to Miami, Florida." I wasn't the only person to hear about the offer but one of the few to phone and request details. The courier service offered an airline ticket to anyone willing to carry a bag of mail to the States.

The deal was tantalizingly simple: meet the company representative at the airport, be given a duffel bag of documents and a ticket. Check the bag when you check in for the flight. Retrieve the bag in Miami before you make your connection. Give it to the uniformed courier representative, who'll await you beyond customs.

No company makes such offers anymore. But this was 1985—years before intense airport security. My dad was dying of ALS, airline tickets were expensive, and my checking account was as thin as a Paris supermodel. Free ticket? The offer sounded too good to be true. So I walked away from it.

Many do the same with John 3:16. Millions read the verse. Only a handful trust it. Wary of a catch, perhaps? Not needy enough maybe? Cautioned by guarded friends?

MILLIONS READ THE VERSE. ONLY A HANDFUL TRUST IT.

2 **Considering the people you know, what do you think their primary reason would be for rejecting the John 3:16 offer? Check one or write your own.**

- a. I really don't have any desire or need for Jesus and eternal life.
- b. If what I see in the lives of other Christians is what I can expect, I'm not interested.
- c. It really is too good to be true. Surely I have to do more than believe.
- d. My family would reject me at best or kill me at worst.
- e. God isn't real, and heaven and hell are just make-believe.
- f. People would think I'm a fool.

Other: _____

I was skeptical. Other Rio residents saw the same offer. Some read it and smelled a rat. "Don't risk it," one warned me. "Better to buy your own ticket." But I couldn't afford a ticket.

Each call to Mom had worse news. "Back in the hospital."

"Unable to breathe without oxygen."

"The doctor says it's time to call hospice."

So I revisited the flyer. Desperation heightened my interest.

Doesn't it always? When he asks for a divorce or she says, "It's over." When the coroner calls, the kids rebel, or the finances collapse. When desperation typhoons into your world, God's offer of a free flight home demands a second look.

John 3:16 morphs from a nice verse to a life vest.

JOHN 3:16 MORPHS FROM A NICE VERSE TO A LIFE VEST.

Some of you are wearing it. You can recount the day you put it on. For you, the passage comforts like your favorite blanket:

- God so loved …
- believes in him …
- shall not perish …
- eternal life.

These words have kept you company through multiple windswept winters. I pray they warm you through the ones that remain.

Others still study the flyer. Still pondering the possibility, wrestling with the promise. One day wondering what kind of fool offer this is, the next wondering what kind of fool would turn it down.

3 **Which of these two conditions best describes you?**
- a. I have believed Jesus and have eternal life.
- b. I'm still wondering, waiting, wavering, wrestling with the promise.

If you're still waiting to believe, I urge you—don't walk away from this one. Who else can get you home? Who else has turned His grave into a changing closet and offered to do the same with yours? Take Jesus' offer. Get on board. You don't want to miss this chance to see your Father.

I didn't. I called the company and signed up. Denalyn drove me to the airport. I found the courier employee, accepted the passage, checked the bag, and took my seat on the plane, smiling as though I'd just found a forgotten gift under the Christmas tree.

Do likewise. You don't need to go to the airport, but you do need to give God your answer: "Christ will live in you as you open the door and invite him in" (Eph. 3:17, NKJV). Say yes to Him. Your prayer needs no eloquence, just honesty.

Father, I believe You love this world. You gave Your one and only Son so that I can live forever with You. Apart from You I die. With You I live. I choose life. I choose You.

YOU DON'T WANT TO MISS THIS CHANCE TO SEE YOUR FATHER.

If you aren't sure you've told Him, you haven't. We can't get on board and not know it. Nor can we get on board and hide it. No stowaways permitted.

- Christ-followers go public with their belief.
- We turn from bad behavior to good (repentance).
- We stop following our passions and salute our new Captain (confession).
- We publicly demonstrate our devotion (baptism) (see Rom. 10:9; Acts 26:20; 2:38).

We don't keep our choice a secret. Why would we?

Thanks to the courier folks, I was present at my father's death.

Thanks to God, He'll be present at yours. He cares too much not to be. Believe in Him, and you will not perish.

YOUR CONVERSATION WITH GOD

As you conclude these daily conversations with God, find a place away from distractions. Call on God for a one-on-one encounter. Talk to Him. Reflect on the message of grace. Have you truly embraced this passage? Share with God your fears, desires, and hopes. He's listening; He cares; He is with you always even to the end of earth's existence.

ACTS 26:20

"I preached that they should repent and turn to God and prove their repentance by their deeds."

Jesus, I want to join the parade of hope. I want to be released from moments of fear, insecurity, and doom. I want to publicly acknowledge You as my King. Lord Jesus Christ, Son of God, I want to change the world, even if it is just moment by moment, inch by inch, life by life. I want to live a life of grace and meaning because I know that it is what You died for. Praise You, Savior Jesus, for the parade of hope. Let freedom and grace and mercy ring out in my life.

THE 3:16 LIFE

A PARADE OF HOPE

day five

MY PERSONAL
DARK-DAY STORIES

1 Which of the following dark days have you experienced?

- Death of a spouse or child
- Job loss
- Death of a close friend
- Divorce
- Death of a parent
- Rape
- Death of a dream
- Abuse
- Extended unemployment
- Addiction
- Personal/family disabilities
- Personal/family illness
- Imprisonment
- Victim of crime
- Suicide of a friend or family member
- Loss of home or business to fire, flood, or other disaster
- Car accident in which you/others were seriously injured

Other: _____

2 When the events you identified above first occurred, what emotions did you experience?

- Love of friends
- God's peace
- Love of family
- Depression
- Understanding
- Guilt
- Hope
- Shame
- God's presence
- Abandonment
- Fear
- Anger
- Despair
- Numbness
- Hopelessness
- Loss
- Sorrow
- Support from church

3 If you had to select one day as the time you felt the most hopeless in all your life, what day would it be? Use the journal space on page 135 to write notes, words, phrases, a poem, or a prayer to tell one of your dark-day stories. What happened? How did you feel and respond?

_____

_____

_____

_____

_____

_____

_____

_____

_____

_____

_____

_____

_____

YOUR CONVERSATION WITH GOD

Talk to God about your dark-day experiences. Ask Him to show you any areas of unresolved grief, unhealed hurt, or unmended relationship that you may be carrying. Thank Him and praise Him for His love and power. He loves you as you are, but He loves you too much to leave you as you are.

GOD LOVES

d a y   f i v e

MY B.C. STORY

B.C.—Before Christ. The Scriptures say, "If anyone is in Christ, he is a new creation; the old has gone, the new has come! All this is from God, who reconciled us to himself through Christ" (2 Cor. 5:17-18). Everyone has a before-Christ life, and some may still be living in it.

1 Honestly describe what that life was (or is) like before Christ. Think about …

- Sinful activities, habits, attitudes, or actions that characterized your life
- Lack of purpose, meaning, direction, joy, or fulfillment
- Lack of meaningful relationships or broken relationships
- Suffering from the consequences of your sin
- Selfishness—a self-directed life rather than a God-directed one
- Opposition to God and His people
- Addictions that left you out of control
- Religious activity without the reality of a relationship with Christ—goodness without godliness
- Passions and ambitions for things that have no lasting value
- Counsel from others about your rebellion and wayward life
- Feelings of darkness, fear, depression, loneliness, despair, hopelessness, shame, or guilt

2 Use the journal space on pages 137–39 to write notes, words, phrases, a poem, or a story to describe your life before you experienced new life in Christ. Conclude with a two- or three-sentence summary of your before-Christ story.

_____

_____

_____

_____

_____

_____

_____

_____

_____

_____

_____

_____

_____

_____

_____

YOUR CONVERSATION WITH GOD

Talk to God about your B.C. life. Talk about how His care was evident even before you were a committed follower. Tell Him ways you need His help to increasingly realize His new creation. Ask yourself this before God: Are you still living on the B.C. side of life, or can you rejoice with Him that you are now His?

GOD GAVE

day five

THE 3:16 DIFFERENCE

"The thief comes only to steal and kill and destroy; I have come that they may have life, and have it to the full."
JOHN 10:10

"Those God foreknew he also predestined to be conformed to the likeness of his Son, that he might be the firstborn among many brothers."
ROMANS 8:29

"When Christ, who is your life, appears, then you also will appear with him in glory. Put to death, therefore, whatever belongs to your earthly nature: sexual immorality, impurity, lust, evil desires and greed, which is idolatry."
COLOSSIANS 3:4-5

1 Read the Scriptures in the margin and notice the differences between the practices of the old earthly nature and those of the new nature of people who are in Christ and are being transformed into His likeness. The new 3:16 life is different.

FOR THOSE YET TO BELIEVE

2 What are the things in your life you would love to change if God would help accomplish it in you? Use the journal space on pages 141–43 to write notes, words, phrases, or a description of the things you would like to change (like attitudes, behaviors, addictions, relationships, speech, etc.).

FOR THOSE WHO BELIEVE

3 Use the journal space on pages 141–43 to write notes, words, phrases, a poem, or a story to describe the difference Christ has made in your life since you came to believe in Him. Consider answering some of the following.

a. What difference has Christ made in your life since you turned to Him for life? What has changed?

b. Are you living in the full potential of the 3:16 life Christ came to give? Are you increasingly set free from sin (see Rom. 6)? If not, why not?

c. What steps have you taken to grow in your walk with Him?

d. How is God working in your life to make you more like Christ?

_____

_____

_____

_____

_____

_____

_____

_____

_____

_____

_____

_____

YOUR CONVERSATION WITH GOD

Converse with God about how you and He feel about the things that still need to change for you to experience the fullness of the 3:16 life. Thank Him for the things He's already done and celebrate those with Him. Identify and surrender specific areas of your life to Him so He can continue to transform you into the likeness of Christ.

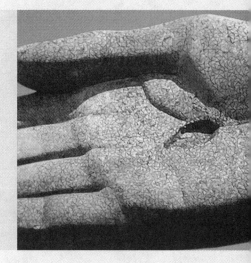

day five

THE CROSSOVER

FOR THOSE YET TO BELIEVE

1 **What are the reasons you are not yet ready to believe in Jesus Christ? Honestly consider the questions or barriers keeping you from choosing to believe. Use the journal space on pages 145–47 to write notes or a description of the questions or barriers. Consider such things as:**

- The cost of following Christ, what changes will be required
- The faith to believe the promise or to trust in the reality of Jesus Christ
- The things others would say or do because you believe
- What you see in the church or other believers who may not be living in the full reality of the new relationship with Christ

FOR THOSE WHO BELIEVE

2 **What's your crossover story? When and how did you choose to move from death to life? Use the journal space on pages 145–47 to write notes, words, phrases, or a description of how you came to "stretch yourself out and rest" on Christ. Consider such things as:**

- When did you first recognize that you needed a Savior?
- When did you first hear the good news God had to offer? Who shared that news with you? What Scriptures were important or meaningful?
- How did God use circumstances or situations to bring you to Himself? Was there a crisis of some kind?
- What obstacles or barriers to belief stood between you and faith in Jesus? How did you overcome or resolve those?

_____

_____

_____

_____

_____

_____

_____

_____

_____

_____

_____

_____

YOUR CONVERSATION WITH GOD

Talk to God about the nature and status of your belief in His Son, Jesus. Bring your deepest questions to Him. Ask God to reveal Himself, answer your questions, and overcome the obstacles that hinder your faith. If you know you belong to Christ, use this time to express your gratitude to God for the people and circumstances that led you to Him.

WE LIVE

day five

MY 3:16 STORY

"All have sinned and fall short of the glory of God."
ROMANS 3:23

"The wages of sin is death, but the gift of God is eternal life in Christ Jesus our Lord."
ROMANS 6:23

"God demonstrates his own love for us in this: While we were still sinners, Christ died for us."
ROMANS. 5:8

"If you confess with your mouth, 'Jesus is Lord,' and believe in your heart that God raised him from the dead, you will be saved. For it is with your heart that you believe and are justified, and it is with your mouth that you confess and are saved. Everyone who calls on the name of the Lord will be saved."
ROMANS 10:9-10,13

FOR THOSE YET TO BELIEVE

1 Read the Scriptures in the margin. They describe our need for a Savior and invite a response.

2 Use the journal space on pages 149–51 to write notes, words, phrases, or a description of the reasons you would not want to choose hell as your destiny. List reasons you would want life with Jesus Christ now and heaven for all eternity. Summarize any struggles that may still keep you from choosing life.

FOR THOSE WHO BELIEVE

3 Use the journal space on pages 149–51 to write your 3:16 story. Include what life was like before Christ, what brought you to faith, how you responded to the 3:16 invitation, and what difference Christ has made in your life since then. Feel free to use prose; poetry; a song/music; a picture/drawing/painting; a timeline; a collage of pictures (real or symbolic); a sculpture; an audio CD; a video testimony, interview, or documentary; and so forth. Be prepared to share your 3:16 story with your group during the next session.

_____
_____
_____
_____
_____
_____
_____
_____
_____
_____
_____
_____

YOUR CONVERSATION WITH GOD

Talk to God about what you've heard from Him and your experiences over the past five weeks. Share your thoughts and feelings with Him. Ask how He wants you to respond and with whom you might share this message of hope, love, and life.

3:16 PRAYER LIST

List below the names of people who need to hear and believe the message of John 3:16. Include immediate family members, relatives, friends, neighbors, coworkers, associates, acquaintances, or people you know only from afar but who need to trust Christ. Begin praying regularly for God to draw these people to faith in His Son, Jesus Christ. Pray that God will give you an opportunity to share this message and tell your own 3:16 story.

_____

_____

_____

_____

_____

_____

_____

_____

_____

_____

_____

_____

_____

LEADER GUIDE

The following pages will help you prepare for and conduct a six-session group study of *3:16 The Church Experience Workbook.*

YOUR ROLE AS GROUP LEADER

You do not have to be a content expert to lead this Bible study. Your role is more that of a facilitator. Max Lucado will provide inspiring messages from God's Word each week in a DVD segment. During the week participants will study this workbook and complete the interactive learning activities and prayer experiences. They will begin to develop their own 3:16 stories. Through these content segments and learning experiences, participants will be primed and ready to discuss the messages and to share personal insights and experiences.

The three-page spread at the beginning of each week provides a practical guide for your group session. On those pages you will find—

- a discussion guide for the previous week's study;
- DVD message notes for the teaching segment by Max Lucado;
- suggestions to guide group discussion and sharing in response to the DVD message;
- highlights from the upcoming week's study.

As time permits, you will close each session with a 3:16 story (testimony) from the DVD. In many cases those segments, together with times to pray, will fill your group session. If you have more time, you may choose to use some of the additional suggestions on the pages that follow. By using these resources, you can be a lead learner along with the other group participants. You could even share leadership if desired or necessary.

Pray

Because this is a spiritual process in which God is involved, pray for His leadership and involvement. Pray for wisdom. Pray that God will draw participants into the study for their benefit and His kingdom work. Pray that God will strengthen believers and call them to active duty in the harvest. Pray that those who have not yet believed in Christ will be drawn and compelled by God's Spirit to believe.

Set a Time and Place for Group Sessions

Group sessions can take place any time that is convenient for participants—Sundays, weekdays, or Saturdays; daytime or evening. We recommend 90-minute sessions so you will have adequate time to view the DVD segments

(25 to 30 minutes each week) and process what God has taught and done during the week. You could try shorter sessions, but you will likely find yourself pressed for time for members to adequately process what they are learning. Because the DVD messages by Max Lucado are a primary source of the content for the study, you must use the DVD messages with the workbook to gain the most from this study.

Groups may meet at the church building, in homes or apartments, in a community meeting room, in a workplace before or after work or over lunch, in a school, or almost anyplace. The availability of a monitor (or projector) and DVD player, sufficient space, and enough privacy to prevent interruption are the primary factors that may limit your choice of locations. Consider nontraditional places if members want to use this as an outreach opportunity.

Determine Fees (If Any)

Each participant will need a workbook for the group study. Determine the cost for participants so you can mention the cost in advertising the course. Usually, people are more faithful to use the workbook and attend the group sessions when they have made a personal investment in the resource. Be prepared to provide partial or complete scholarships when needed so no one will be prohibited from the study because of financial limitations.

Group Size

The very best small-group dynamics take place in groups of 8 to 15 members who remain consistent over time (in this case six sessions). Smaller groups may be too intimate for some. If members know and trust one another, smaller groups will be satisfactory. Larger groups are too big to allow everyone to participate adequately. If you are really serious about enabling people to experience the depth of this message, you don't want to have spectators. If you have more than 15, consider dividing into multiple groups.

If your church has multiple groups meeting at the same time at church, you may choose to watch the DVD messages as a large group and divide into smaller groups for content discussion and response to the DVD messages. If you use this format, consider keeping participants in the same small group each week. Don't require people to get acquainted and develop new relationships each week. They need to develop trust for sharing deeper thoughts and feelings as the study progresses.

Enlist Participants

Use your church's normal channels to advertise this study: bulletins, posters, newsletters, Power-Point® slides before the service, announcements, church Web site, and so forth. DVD 1 includes a promotional segment (2 min., 15 sec.) that will introduce people to 3:16 and invite their participation. Another 3:16 promotional segment titled "What If?" is included on the leader CD-ROM in a computer movie format. You may share the "What If?" file by e-mail if you wish. You have permission to do so.

We assume that most participants in *3:16 The Church Experience* will already have a saving relationship with Jesus Christ. However, you need not limit the group to believers only. Those who have not yet believed need to be introduced to this message also. This might be the opportunity when they encounter the living God and choose to trust Christ. In several places Max extends an invitation for people to do so. However, you may consider using the workbooks and "The Church Experience" to introduce this message to church members. Once they have reviewed God's work in their lives and prepared their own 3:16 stories, you can pray about ways to best use the variety of 3:16 resources to share the gospel with friends, relatives, neighbors, and others in your community who have not yet believed in Jesus Christ.

Order Resources

Each participant will need a workbook (item 005115511). Because each person will need to give individual responses to the learning activities and make journal entries for "The 3:16 Life," a married couple will need to have two workbooks instead of sharing one copy. You will also need one leader kit (item 005035514) for your church or group. The kit includes a special leader CD-ROM, one copy of this workbook, a copy of *3:16 The Numbers of Hope* hardback book, two DVDs with weekly teaching segments and testimonies (3:16 stories) plus a promotional segment, a listening-music CD for *3:16 The Worship Musical*, and other sample 3:16 resources. The CD-ROM contains an administration guide and other leader helps for a retreat and a churchwide 3:16 campaign.

Order resources by writing to LifeWay Church Resources Customer Service; One LifeWay Plaza; Nashville, TN 37234-0113; faxing (615) 251-5933; phoning toll free (800) 458-2772; ordering online at *www. lifeway.com*; e-mailing *orderentry@ lifeway.com;* or visiting a LifeWay Christian Store.

Web Sites

As the momentum grows, ideas are generated, and new 3:16 resources are released, you can stay up-to-date by checking the following Web sites: *www.lifeway.com/316* (hosted by LifeWay Christian Resources) and *www.threesixteen.net* (hosted by Thomas Nelson and Max Lucado). As they become available, new resources, video downloads, and other tools to enrich your experience of this message and to share it with others will be added to the sites.

Secure Equipment and Supplies

In addition to the workbooks and the leader kit, secure the following equipment and supplies for use during the sessions.

- Monitor (or projector) and DVD player
- Name tags and markers
- Marker board or chart paper and markers
- Extra pens or pencils
- Roster for keeping attendance records
- Index cards for members' contact information

Preview Workbook and DVD Messages

You may prefer to study the entire workbook and view all of the DVD messages before beginning the study with your group. The leader kit also gives suggestions for a churchwide leadership retreat to introduce the study to your leaders in a concentrated time. However, you may study one week ahead of your group and have a good experience. Before the first session, read "Introducing 3:16" (pp. 5–6), study week 1 (pp. 7–24), and view session 1 on the DVD. Be prepared to explain the way members will use this workbook to complete five daily devotionals each week.

Prepare to Introduce Max Lucado

Read "Introducing Max Lucado" on page 4 and be prepared to introduce Max to your group at the first session. If you would like to find out more about his ministries, you can visit his Web site at *www.maxlucado.com.* Max shares his own 3:16 story in conjunction with session 6 on DVD 2. You might want to play that segment (02:12) as part of your introduction.

Session Plans

In the following plans you will find suggestions for preparations to make before the session. The first session provides an introduction to the study. It will help your members get acquainted with one another and become familiar with the upcoming study. Then they will listen to Max's introductory message on John 3:16. Sessions 2–6 are divided into two relatively equal parts:

- Part 1—Discussion of the previous week's devotionals
- Part 2—Viewing and discussing the DVD message from Max and the related 3:16 story

We highly recommend a 90-minute session as a minimum time for the study each week. If you have a 90-minute session, each part should take about 45 minutes. If you have more or less time, adjust the times accordingly. If you have only one hour, use 20 minutes for part 1 and 40 minutes for part 2.

If tried to use all of the suggested activities in the following session plans, you would not be able to complete them in a 90-minute session. Review the suggestions and select the activities and questions you believe will be most helpful to your group. Don't get frustrated by not finishing everything. Pray that the Holy Spirit will guide you in the selection. Pay attention to His leadership in the session if you need to change plans based on the responses and needs of the group. Pay attention to your group members more than the agenda.

GROUP SESSION 1 • A PARADE OF HOPE

This first session is your introductory session to this study of Max Lucado's *3:16 The Church Experience*. During this session participants will be introduced to the study by a DVD segment from Max Lucado. They will get acquainted with other members of the small group, receive their workbooks, and preview the first week's devotionals.

BEFORE THE SESSION

■ 1. Set up the room so members can view the DVD segment. Keep it flexible enough so members can move around to face one another for discussion and sharing times.

■ 2. Check the monitor (or projector) and DVD player to make sure they are working properly. Adjust the volume. Cue your DVD to the message for "Session 1: A Parade of Hope."

■ 3. On a marker board or chart paper, list the information you want to collect from each member: name, mailing address, e-mail address, phone numbers, and so forth.

■ 4. Provide name tags, markers, index cards, and pencils/pens.

■ 5. Prepare a roster of persons who have registered for the class. If they have not preregistered, be prepared to complete the roster as participants arrive.

■ 6. Set out copies of *3:16 The Church Experience Workbook* and prepare to collect fees.

■ 7. Prepare to introduce the components of the workbook and course (pp. 5–6), and prepare to introduce Max Lucado (p. 4).

DURING THE SESSION, PART 1
(45 minutes)

1. As members arrive, provide name tags and collect contact information you need on the index cards.

2. Check off participants on the roster and add those who have not preregistered.

3. Provide a copy of the workbook and collect fees (if any).

4. Open with a prayer that God will use this study to help every participant experience the full reality of the life promised in John 3:16.

5. Introduce participants to the components of the workbook by presenting the content of "Introducing 3:16" on pages 5–6. Guide members to locate the items listed in the margin on page 5.

6. Explain that group sessions once each week will include a discussion of the previous week's workbook content and listening to Max's message for the coming week's study.

7. Participants will study devotionals in the workbook five days each week.

8. Guide introductions by asking members to share the information in activity 1 on page 8.

   [1. Introduce yourself to the group by sharing: (1) your name and brief information about your family; (2) where you spend most of your time during the week (home, school, business); and (3) why you chose to participate in this study.]

9. As time permits, invite members to respond to activities 2 and 3 on page 8.

   [2. We will study the parade of hope found in John 3:16, which stands in sharp contrast to times of fear, terror, loss, or despair. How did you feel when you received news of the terrorist attacks on September 11, 2001? Were you directly affected by the loss of a friend or a loved one and, if so, how?]

   [3. Now briefly share memories of *one* of these other historic dark days. (See p. 8.)]

DURING THE SESSION, PART 2
(45 minutes)

1. Using the information on page 4, introduce Max Lucado.

2. Play the DVD message "Session 1: A Parade of Hope" (21:22). Invite members to follow the notes on the listening guide on page 9 and fill in the blanks. (Answers to the blanks in the message notes are found at the bottom of the listening guide each week. Also point out that Scriptures referenced in the message are also included at the bottom of the listening guide.)

3. Following the DVD message, use the Group Response questions on page 9 to discuss the message in small groups of six to eight members.

4. Play the 3:16 story by Pastor Joseph Cortese (04:05) on DVD 1. Ask: *What statement in this 3:16 story was most encouraging or meaningful to you and why?*

5. Close with a prayer that God will reveal Himself and His hope and life to every person in your group. Pray that all group members will experience growth and transformation during the coming weeks.

6. Remind members to complete the devotionals in the workbook prior to the next session.

GROUP SESSION 2 • GOD LOVES

BEFORE THE SESSION

1. Set up the room and check the DVD player to make sure it is working properly.

2. Cue DVD 1 to play session 2.

3. Review the following session plans and determine which questions or activities will be most helpful to your group if time permits you to use them.

4. Review activity B below. Prepare to share your own dark-day story *briefly* as a model of the time frame and transparency desired.

DURING THE SESSION, PART 1
(45 minutes)

A. Prayer. Begin the session with a prayer that the Lord will open the minds and hearts of your members to understand the full dimensions of God's love for them.

B. The 3:16 Life. Ask members to turn to pages 134–35. Invite some volunteers who are willing to *briefly* (two to three minutes) share with the group either one of their own dark-day stories (activities 1 and 2) or their most hopeless day (#3). Set an example for the time frame and depth of sharing by telling your own story. As members share, decide whether the hurt or pain is still sufficient to warrant your

taking time for group members to pray for the person's healing and restoration. [Note: this is intended as a group-building exercise. Don't get in such a hurry that you miss the benefit of this sharing time. You may not have much time left for the following discussion, but this week that's OK.]

C. Group Review. Use some or all of the following questions and sharing activities from the Group Review for week 1 on page 26.

1. Briefly describe a time when you got lost at night. What were the circumstances, and how did you feel?

2. What's the difference between following a religious system and following Jesus? Share some of your thoughts from activity 2 (p. 14).

3. Nicodemus faced risks and struggles in coming to Jesus, just as many people do today. In your opinion, what drove Nicodemus to come to Jesus by night? Similarly, what might drive you and others to "come to Jesus at night"? (activities 5 and 6, p. 16).

4. What would you say if you had the opportunity to tell Jesus how much His work of the new birth means to you? Start with the ideas you jotted down in the margin for activity 6 on page 20.

5. Why do you think John 3:16 inspired Newton to describe God's grace as "amazing" (activity 4, p. 23)? As you feel free to do so, share a time when God absolutely amazed you with His grace.

D. Optional Sharing and Discussion. As time permits, use some of the following activities.

1. Share and explain your responses to the following activities.

 ■ Activity 2, page 11. Describe a time when you experienced great disappointment.

 ■ Activity 4, page 12. Do you need some hope right now? If so, how may we pray for you? [Then pray.]

 ■ Activity 1, page 22. What do you think is the most unlovable thing about the world and why?

 ■ Activity 3, page 23. What do you think is the most common perception about God and why?

 ■ Activity 6, page 24. How would you explain to a friend what it means to stretch out on Christ and rest?

2. Review the following content.

 ■ What are some of the things Jesus did that disrupted the comfortable world of the religious leaders of His day (p. 15)?

 ■ What did Jesus mean by the term *born again* (day 3, pp. 18–21)?

3. Discuss the following questions.

 ■ Of all the verses in the Bible, why do you think John 3:16 has become such an important verse to Christians?

 ■ How have your conversations with God been meaningful to you this week?

DURING THE SESSION, PART 2
(45 minutes)

1. Play the DVD message "Session 2: God Loves" (29:31). Invite members to follow the notes on the listening guide on pages 26–27 and fill in the blanks.

2. Following the DVD message, use the Group Response questions on page 27 to discuss the message in small groups of six to eight members.

3. Play the 3:16 story by Christine Peña on DVD 1. Ask: *What statement in this 3:16 story was most meaningful to you and why? Do you know someone who needs to hear this story? If so, who and why? Record his or her name on your 3:16 prayer list on pages 152–53.*

4. Close the session with prayer. Invite members to pray sentence prayers of praise and thanksgiving to God for His great love for us and for this world.

3:16

GROUP SESSION 3 • GOD GAVE

BEFORE THE SESSION

1. Set up the room and check the DVD player to make sure it is working properly.
2. Cue DVD 1 to play session 3.
3. Review the following session plans and determine which questions or activities will be most helpful to your group if time permits you to use them.
4. Enlist a member to plan to lead the closing prayer. Ask him or her to sum up the group's heart responses to this message and express them to the Lord.

DURING THE SESSION, PART 1
(45 minutes)

A. Prayer. Open the session with prayer. Thank the Lord that He loved us enough that He didn't leave us as we once were. Thank Him for what He has done for us through Christ. Ask Him to guide your understanding of His 3:16 promise.

B. Group Review. Use some or all of the following questions and sharing activities from the Group Review for week 2 on page 50.

1. Denalyn was kept off a plane because a pilot didn't receive an important message from me. Has there been a similar time in your life, when you felt that God wasn't hearing you—and didn't seem too interested in listening?

2. Describe an occasion when you have questioned the "pilot," asking God some tough life questions. How did it go? Look back at your answers to activities 2 and 3 (pp. 30–31).

3. What attribute of God impresses you most (activities 4 and 7, pp. 34–35)? Why? On which one do you most need to focus in your praise and worship?

4. How are you growing in your realization that the God of the universe loves you so much that He is pulling for you? In what ways did you sense His doing so last week? (See activities 5 and 6, p. 35.)

5. Share some of your thoughts about activity 2 on page 38: What part of being tethered to God gives you comfort, and what part of the idea troubles you? What difference does God's perfect love make in your answers?

C. The 3:16 Life. Divide into smaller groups of four to six. Ask members to share their three-sentence summaries of their B.C. (before-Christ) stories (activity 2, p. 136). Ask one member in each group to conclude their time of sharing with prayer. Thank the Lord that these B.C. stories are not the end of your stories.

162

D. Optional Sharing and Discussion. As time permits, guide responses to some of the following activities.

1. Share and explain your responses to the following activities.

  - Activity 6, page 32. For those who had a chance to take your Bible discovery outside, describe your experience meditating on God and the heavens He's created.

  - Activity 8, page 36. Share about a time you did something stupid and what you've experienced of God's grace since then.

  - Activity 8, page 41. What description of God's love was most meaningful to you and why?

2. Review the following content.

  - How would you explain that our sense of right and wrong argues for the existence of God (activity 2, p. 33)?

  - What are some of the attributes of God that cause you to worship Him (pp. 34–35)?

  - What actions can you take to soften your heart (see activity 6, p. 47)?

3. Discuss the following questions.

  - How can you identify whether you have a hard heart, and what is the remedy if you do?

  - How have your conversations with God been meaningful to you this week?

DURING THE SESSION, PART 2
(45 minutes)

1. Play the DVD message "Session 3: God Gave" (30:53). Invite members to follow the notes on the listening guide on pages 50–51 and fill in the blanks.

2. Following the DVD message, use the Group Response questions on page 51 to discuss the message in small groups of six to eight members.

3. Play the 3:16 Story by Anita Garaa (04:00) on DVD 1. Ask: *What statement in this 3:16 story was most meaningful to you and why? Do you know someone who needs to hear this story? If so, who and why? Record his or her name on your 3:16 prayer list on pages 152–53.*

4. Call on the person you enlisted to close the session with prayer.

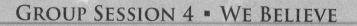

BEFORE THE SESSION

1. Set up the room and check the DVD player to make sure it is working properly.

2. Cue DVD 2 to play session 4.

3. Review the following session plans and determine which questions or activities will be most helpful to your group if time permits you to use them.

DURING THE SESSION, PART 1
(45 minutes)

A. **Prayer.** Begin the session with sentence prayers thanking God for sending His Son. Thank Him for the change Christ has made in your lives.

B. **Group Review.** Use some or all of the following questions and sharing activities from the Group Review of week 3 on page 70.

1. What are some things you wish Jesus, the one and only Revealer, would teach you? Share some things He has already taught you, positively changing your life as a result (activities 5 and 6, pp. 59–60).

2. What are some reasons you think our generation is oddly silent about sin (activity 5, p. 63)? What is an appropriate Christian response?

3. How does Jesus put Himself on the line for you? How do you tend to respond to His great gift (see activities 1–3, p. 66)?

4. In the spiritual rather than the medical sense, what are important distinctions between a heart transplant and a heart swap (see pp. 67–68)?

5. In your opinion, how important to your complete 3:16 story is the part about what Jesus has done for you? Why?

C. **The 3:16 Life.** Invite volunteers to tell about the difference Christ has made in their lives since they first came to Him by faith (activity 3, p. 149).

D. **Optional Sharing and Discussion.** As time permits, guide responses to some of the following activities.

1. Share and explain your responses to the following activities.
   - Activity 6, page 56. How can you acknowledge Christ's supremacy or authority in your life?
   - Activity 1, page 57. What do you need Jesus to reveal to you about the Father?
   - Activity 2, page 62. How did you explain 1 Peter 2:22-24?

2. Review the following content.

- What does "one and only" mean (pp. 54–55)?

- What has Jesus done for *(hyper)* us or "on our behalf" (p. 65)?

3. Discuss the following questions.

- In general, how well are the members of our church living up to the full potential of an abundant life in Christ? What is the evidence that we are or that we are not?

- In what kinds of life situations do you feel "lost in the streets of Rio" and need to look to Jesus to get your bearings?

- Why do you think God is so uncompromising in His refusal to ignore sin or let it go unpunished?

- What do you think we receive when Christ swaps hearts with us?

- How have your conversations with God been meaningful to you this week?

4. Invite members to pray sentence prayers thanking God for the gift of His Son or for the new heart Jesus gives when He swaps hearts with us.

DURING THE SESSION, PART 2
(45 minutes)

1. Play the DVD message "Session 4: We Believe" (27:44). Invite members to follow the notes on the listening guide on pages 70–71 and fill in the blanks.

2. Following the DVD message, use the Group Response questions on page 71 to discuss the message in small groups of six to eight members.

3. Play the 3:16 story by Liem Nyguen (04:24) on DVD 2. Ask: *What statement in this 3:16 story was most meaningful to you and why? Do you know someone who needs to hear this story? If so, who and why? Record his or her name on your 3:16 prayer list on pages 152–53.*

4. Close the session with prayer. Invite volunteers to pray specifically for persons in their circles of influence who need to believe in Jesus Christ.

GROUP SESSION 5 ▪ WE LIVE

BEFORE THE SESSION

▪ 1. Set up the room and check the DVD player to make sure it is working properly.

▪ 2. Cue DVD 2 to play session 5.

▪ 3. Review the following session plans and determine which questions or activities will be most helpful to your group if time permits you to use them.

▪ 4. Think about how you will guide people to share their 3:16 stories in session 6 (see #5 at the end of this session). If you anticipate needing more time, you may want to consider planning an extra session and fellowship just for telling your 3:16 stories. If you decide to do so, start planning now.

DURING THE SESSION, PART 1
(45 minutes)

A. Prayer. Begin the session by inviting members to pray sentence prayers confessing truths they believe about Jesus Christ, who He is, and what He has done for them.

B. Group Review. Use some or all of the following questions and sharing activities from the Group Review for week 4 on page 90.

▪ 1. Discuss your responses to this question from day 1 (p. 74): Have you ever been in a situation in which you trusted someone with your safety or your life? Why do you think this is a struggle for some people?

▪ 2. If someone walked into the room right now and asked how you know for certain you have eternal life, how would you respond? How has your understanding of *belief* changed this week?

▪ 3. Who helped you understand that you can't save you, and what did that person do to help you (based on p. 81)? Whom are you helping to come to the same personal understanding? Choose a partner and pray together by name for the salvation of friends and for each other as you share God's good news.

▪ 4. How would you answer someone who tells you, "All roads lead to heaven" (see activity 5, p. 82)?

▪ 5. Turn to page 87 and discuss your responses to activity 5.

C. The 3:16 Life. Divide into smaller groups of four to six members. Ask members to share their responses to either activity 1 or activity 2 on page 144. Ask one member from each group to respond to the Lord in prayer for their group, based on what has been shared.

D. Optional Sharing and Discussion. As time permits, guide responses to some of the following activities.

1. Review the following content.
   - What are some reasons Jesus can be trusted (activity 4, p. 75)?
   - What is God's way to eternal life (activity 3, p. 77)?

2. Discuss the following questions.
   - Why do you think humans would rather work to be right with God than believe?
   - How have your conversations with God been meaningful to you this week?

DURING THE SESSION, PART 2
(45 minutes)

1. Play the DVD message "Session 5: We Live" (31:23). Invite members to follow the notes on the listening guide on pages 90–91 and fill in the blanks.

2. Following the DVD message, use the Group Response questions on page 91 to discuss the message in small groups of six to eight members.

3. Play the 3:16 story by Chris Bartella (06:47) on DVD 2. Ask: *What statement in this 3:16 Story was most meaningful to you and why? Do you know someone who needs to hear this story? If so, who and why? Record his or her name on your 3:16 prayer list on pages 152–53.*

4. Invite members to pray for the many people in your own community and around the world who have not yet believed in Jesus Christ and are headed to an eternity without Him. Pray that God will empower you and your church to share the good news of the 3:16 promise with great fruitfulness. Close the prayer time by praying for your group members. Pray that the Lord will guide them as they process their own response to the Lord this week and prepare their 3:16 stories.

5. Before dismissing, explain that day 5 this week will guide members to prepare their own 3:16 stories (p. 148). They will be given permission to use a variety of media to tell their story, such as prose; poetry; a song/ music; a picture/drawing/painting; a time-line; a collage of pictures (real or symbolic); a sculpture; an audio CD; a video testimony, interview, or documentary; and so forth. Ask members to be prepared to share their 3:16 stories next week. Explain, however, that time may limit how many will be able to share their stories with the whole group.

GROUP SESSION 6 · GOD'S WHOEVER POLICY

BEFORE THE SESSION

1. Set up the room and check the DVD player to make sure it is working properly.

2. Cue DVD 2 to play session 6.

3. Plan how you will ask members to share their 3:16 stories. If you anticipate that some may have audio or video stories to share, provide the equipment needed. Anticipate that this may take more time than normal for The 3:16 Life segment of the session. If your group is large, divide into smaller groups so everyone will have an opportunity to tell their story. If you have multiple groups, you may need to limit the smaller-group sharing to oral stories (rather than audio or video). In that case choose one or two 3:16 stories in electronic form to share with the larger group.

4. Prepare to share your own 3:16 story as a model for others.

5. Review the following session plans and determine which questions or activities will be most helpful to your group. Be sure to allow adequate time for prayer at the conclusion of the session.

DURING THE SESSION, PART 1
(45 minutes)

A. **Prayer.** Begin the session with prayer, thanking God that He has a whoever policy that includes everyone in your group. Pray that He will be magnified as you tell your 3:16 stories.

B. **The 3:16 Life.** Invite those who are willing to share their 3:16 stories in whatever format they have prepared them. Use smaller groups of four to six if necessary so everyone will have an opportunity to tell their story.

C. **Group Review.** Use some or all of the following questions and sharing activities from the Group Review for week 5 on page 116.

1. What common perceptions of hell did you identify (activity 5, p. 94)? Why do you think some people prefer to delude themselves with these sanitized versions rather than believe in the real hell? What have you learned about heaven or hell this week that has been most life-changing?

2. How do you sense God leading you to guide others to face death—as well as the everyday struggles of life—with faith and joy? Share your thoughts from activity 8 (p. 101). What does it mean to you that Satan's "days are numbered" (see p. 104)?

3. What are some common reservations about heaven? How did Jesus address these concerns (pp. 102–3)? What do you most anticipate about heaven?

4. How does the phrase "because He's been there" give you life and hope (p. 113)?

D. Optional Sharing and Discussion. As time permits, guide responses to some of the following activities.

1. Share and explain your responses to the following activities.

- Activity 2, page 98. What continuing evil practice would horrify you most about hell? Why?

- Activity 5, page 99. Which description of hell is the most spine-chilling for you? Why?

2. Review the following content.

- What are the truths about existence in hell (days 1 and 2)?

- What are the truths about existence in heaven (day 3)?

3. Discuss the following questions.

- Why can't we accuse God of unfairness for punishing people in hell?

- Why do you think God wants us to understand hell as well as heaven (activity 7, p. 96)?

- What characteristics of heaven make it most appealing to you?

- How have your conversations with God been meaningful to you this week?

DURING THE SESSION, PART 2
(45 minutes)

1. Play the DVD message "Session 6: God's Whoever Policy" (31:28). Invite members to follow the notes on the listening guide on pages 116–17 and fill in the blanks.

2. Following the DVD message, use the Group Response questions on page 117 to discuss the message in small groups of six to eight.

3. Play the 3:16 story by Max Lucado (02:12) on DVD 2. Ask: *What statement in this 3:16 story was most meaningful to you and why? Do you know someone who needs to hear this story? If so, who and why? Record his or her name on your 3:16 prayer list on pages 152–53.*

4. Explain that this is the final session of your study together. Week 6 in the workbook will help members review and further respond to the message of God's whoever policy.

4. Close your study with a time of prayer. Invite members to pray conversationally by expressing what they want to say to the Lord. Pray especially for a season of harvest in which many in your community and circles of influence will place their belief in Jesus Christ. Close the prayer time by praying for and commissioning these members to go forth boldly to share the good news of 3:16 with the people around them.

ENDNOTES

WEEK 2

1. Lee Strobel, *The Case for a Creator* (Grand Rapids: Zondervan, 2005).

2. Bill Tucker, speech, Oak Hills Church men's conference, May 3, 2003.

3. R. Laird Harris, Gleason Archer, and Bruce K. Waltke, eds., *Theological Workbook of the Old Testament,* vol. 1 (Chicago: Moody, 1980), 332, quoted in John Feinberg, gen ed., *No One like Him: The Dosctrine of God* (Wheaton, IL: Crossway Books, 2001), 349.

4. C.S. Lewis, *The World's Last Night and Other Essays,* "The World's Last Night" (1952), 109, as quoted in *The Quotable Lewis,* ed. Wayne Martindale and Jerry Root (Carol Stream, IL: Tyndale, 1990), 400.

5. Thomas Maeder, "A Few Hundred People Turned to Bone," *The Atlantic Monthly* [online], Feburary 1998 [accessed 8 August 2007]. Available from the Internet: *www.theatlantic.com.*

WEEK 3

1. "New Seven Wonders of the World voted in by the world," Science Buzz [online], July 8, 2007 [accessed 6 August 2007]. Available from the Internet: *www.smm.org/buzz.*

"Statue of Christ the Redeemer history & pictures," Copacabana.info [online], [accessed 6 August 2007]. Available from the Internet: *www.copacabana.info.*

2. Charles Colson, *How Now Shall We Live? Adult Member Book* (Nashville: LifeWay Press, 2000).

3. Next Bible [online], 2005, s.v. "huper." [accessed 25 September 2007]. Available from the Internet: *net.bible.org.*

4. Adapted from Steven Vryhof, "Crash Helmets and Church Bells," *Perspectives,* August–September 2000, 3, quoted in Leanne Van Dyk, *Believing in Jesus Christ* (Louisville, KY: Geneva Press, 2002), 109–10.

WEEK 5

1. James Denney, *Studies in Theology* (London: Hodder and Stoughton, 1904), 255, as quoted in Bruce Demarest, *The Cross and Salvation: The Doctrine of Salvation* (Wheaton, IL: Crossway Books, 1997), 31.

2. Thomas Vincent, *Christ's Certain and Sudden Appearance to Judgment,* quoted in Eryl Davies, *The Wrath of God* (Evangelical Press of Wales), 50, quoted in John Blanchard,

Whatever Happened to Hell? (Wheaton, IL: Crossway Books, 1995), 145.

3. C. S. Lewis, *The Problem of Pain* (New York: MacMillan, 1962), 127, quoted in Blanchard, *Whatever Happened to Hell?* 152.

4. Randy Alcorn, *Heaven* (Wheaton, IL: Tyndale House, 2004), 6–7.

5. Ibid., 393.

6. Randy Alcorn, *Heaven* (Nashville: LifeWay Press, 2006).

7. Robert Strand, *Moments for Mothers* (Green Forest, AR: New Leaf Press, 1996), excerpted in Jack Canfield and others, *A Fourth Course of Chicken Soup for the Soul: 101 More Stories to Open the Heart and Rekindle the Spirit* (Deerfield Beach, FL: Health Communications, 1997), 200–201.

8. Vine, *Expository Dictionary of New Testament Words,* 676.

9. Blanchard, *Whatever Happened to Hell?* 54.

most popular English translation of the day, the King James Version: "For God so loved the world, that he gave his only begotten Son, that whosoever believeth in him should not perish, but have everlasting life."

2. Larry Dixon, *The Other Side of the Good News* (Wheaton, IL: Victor Books, 1992), 133.

3. Blue Letter Bible, "Dictionary and Word Search for *diaskorpizo* (Strong's 1287)," Blue Letter Bible [online], 1996–2007, [accessed 8 August 2007]. Available from the Internet: *wwwblueletterbible.org.*

WEEK 6

1. Francis William Boreham, *A Handful Of Stars,* quoted in Stanley Barnes, comp., *Sermons on John 3:16* (Greenville, SC: Emerald House Group, 1999), 19–20. The wording of the verse probably followed the

316

172

CHRISTIAN GR🌍WTH STUDY PLAN

In the Christian Growth Study Plan *3:16 The Church Experience Workbook* is a resource for course credit in the subject area Church and Bible Studies in the Christian Growth category of plans. To receive credit, read the book; complete the learning activities; attend group sessions; show your work to your pastor, a staff member, or a church leader; then complete this form. This page may be duplicated. Send the completed form to:

Christian Growth Study Plan; One LifeWay Plaza; Nashville, TN 37234-0117; fax (615) 251-5067; e-mail *cgspnet@lifeway.com*

For information about the Christian Growth Study Plan, refer to the current *Christian Growth Study Plan Catalog,* located online at *www.lifeway.com/cgsp*. If you do not have access to the Internet, contact the Christian Growth Study Plan office, (800) 968-5519, for the specific plan you need for your ministry.

3:16 The Church Experience Workbook
COURSE NUMBER: CG-1321

PARTICIPANT INFORMATION

Social Security Number (USA ONLY-optional)	Personal CGSP Number*	Date of Birth (MONTH, DAY, YEAR)
Name (First, Middle, Last)		Home Phone
Address (Street, Route, or P.O. Box)	City, State, or Province	Zip/Postal Code
Email Address for CGSP use		

Please check appropriate box: ❑ Resource purchased by church ❑ Resource purchased by self ❑ Other

CHURCH INFORMATION

Church Name		
Address (Street, Route, or P.O. Box)	City, State, or Province	Zip/Postal Code

CHANGE REQUEST ONLY

☐ Former Name		
☐ Former Address	City, State, or Province	Zip/Postal Code
☐ Former Church	City, State, or Province	Zip/Postal Code

Signature of Pastor, Conference Leader, or Other Church Leader	Date

*New participants are requested but not required to give SS# and date of birth. Existing participants, please give CGSP# when using SS# for the first time. Thereafter, only one ID# is required. **Mail to:** Christian Growth Study Plan, One LifeWay Plaza, Nashville, TN 37234-0117. Fax: (615)251-5067.

Revised 4-05

3:16

Find these products and more to support your study of *3:16* at your local LifeWay Christian Store or call 1-800-448-8032.

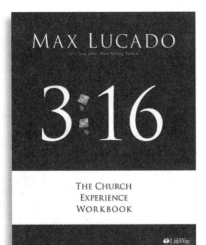

Your Entire Church Can Experience *3:16*

An interactive group experience encouraging church members to live the message of John 3:16 in their lives, in their families, in their communities, and the world.

Workbook 005115511   **Leader Kit** 005035514